PLANS TO PROSPER

How God
Gave Us
Financial
Freedom
Through
Puppies

Karla Green

Foreword by Gary Keesee

Unless otherwise noted, all scriptures are from THE HOLY BIBLE, NEW INTERNATIONAL VERSION®. Copyright© 1973, 1978, 1984, 2011 by Biblica, Inc.™. Used by permission of Zondervan

Scripture quotations marked (ESV) are taken from THE HOLY BIBLE, ENGLISH STANDARD VERSION®, Copyright© 2001 by Crossway, a publishing ministry of Good News Publishers. Used by permission.

Scripture quotations marked (KJV) are taken from the KING JAMES VERSION, public domain.

You may contact the author, Karla Green, at the following email address: tkmgreen@hotmail.com

www.willowgreenministries.com

Individuals and church groups may order books from Karla Green directly, or from the publisher. Retailers and wholesalers should order from our distributors. Refer to the Deeper Revelation Books website for distribution information, as well as an online catalog of all our books.

Published by:

Deeper Revelation Books

Revealing "the deep things of God" (1 Cor. 2:10)

P.O. Box 4260

Cleveland, TN 37320 423-478-2843

Website: www.deeperrevelationbooks.org

Email: info@deeperrevelationbooks.org

Deeper Revelation Books assists Christian authors in publishing and distributing their books. Final responsibility for design, content, permissions, editorial accuracy, and doctrinal views, either expressed or implied, belongs to the author.

Dedication

To my husband and best friend, Todd, and my children Mia and Carter, thank you for going on this amazing God-journey together to change our family legacy. Thank you. I love you.

Acknowledgements

A round of applause for ...

Mike Shreve and Vicki Henley at Deeper Revelation Books for your invaluable oversight and directions to create this book.

Kristin Cooney: my amazing editor who somehow made a musician sound like a writer.

Rebekah Zehr and Heather Jennings: my rough draft editors and for your amazing support and encouragement along the process over coffee. I love you ladies!

Pastor Gary Keesee, my online Pastor: for allowing God to use you to speak directly into my life when I needed it and to encourage me to write our God story.

My parents, Paul and Lisa Schamback: thank you for the double portion!

Mia and Carter: my wonderful kids who have helped this family business be a success with their positive attitudes and great work ethic. I love you both very much.

Todd, my high school sweetheart and love. I'm so thankful God brought us together to share this journey and grow together. I love you.

Table of Contents

Foreword

It is an honor to write the Foreword for Karla's new book, *Plans to Prosper.*

I met Karla through an email that came into our ministry describing their current financial condition, being in debt and living with a very tight budget. Using credit cards to make up the difference, she and her husband Todd were frustrated and looking for answers. Drenda and I came out of very severe financial bondage ourselves years ago by learning the financial laws of the kingdom of God and applying them to our lives. Since then we have spent the last thirty years helping thousands discover how to walk financially free in life by applying these same laws of the kingdom to their own situation. Todd and Karla became students of the kingdom, applying the same laws we discovered and reaped the same results we did: complete financial freedom.

Karla does a great job taking you on the journey she and her family took to reach financial freedom. A goal that at one time seemed completely and absolutely impossible suddenly becomes possible with God's help. You will find her story inspiring and informative. Karla is now on a mission, to declare to people everywhere, that they can be free from debt and live the good life that Jesus paid for. Todd and Karla are a testimony of the power of God, power that is available to anyone if they will take the time to learn the laws that govern the kingdom of God.

Gary Keesee
Faith Life Church, New Albany, Ohio
Forward Financial Group
www.faithlifechurch.org
www.garykeesee.com
www.forwardfinancialgroup.com

Introduction

"The thief comes only to steal and kill and destroy. I came that they may have life and have it abundantly." John 10:10 (ESV)

Can you have it all?

A thriving marriage.

Children who walk in peace with one another.

Generous finances.

Excellent health.

A dream home.

Can you have an abundance in all these areas?

Doesn't one area have to be sacrificed for peace in another?

For years I believed that you had to pick and choose which part of life you could find success in. It was a balancing act where some things just couldn't get the attention they needed.

I found that the couples around me in our church and community were struggling with the "balancing act" too. Especially the mothers, who were constantly questioning if they should get a part-time job to help with the family finances even though their hearts were to stay home with their babies. The mothers who have purpose-driven careers were also conflicted stating, "I make good money, but I'm losing my connection with our kids because I'm not home enough to build a relationship." I saw one-income families who struggled to live in a cramped house, raising four kids with one bathroom in order to "make do" because they desired to homeschool.

We pick the "best option under the circumstances," sacrificing for the greater good. We wear many hats and juggle many balls to make it all work. It's exhausting. Tiresome. My friends and I loved God and went to church, but we knew something was missing, especially in our finances.

Gods plan is for us to have an abundant life in every area.

Jesus said in John 10:10 (ESV), *"The thief comes only to steal and kill and destroy. I came that they may have life and have it **abundantly**."*

Jesus made a bold statement; we are to have life and life abundantly, not "just getting by and surviving one more day." After all, God is the Creator of it all … life, marriage, finances, family. But the abundant life was not what we were living. How does it all work "abundantly"?

We needed answers.

CHAPTER ONE

Livin' On Love

"My people are destroyed from lack of knowledge." Hosea 4:6

My husband Todd and I were high school sweethearts. We attended a small public school in northern New York. Our love for music brought us together. We both played alto saxophone in the high school band. Band field trips made for long bus rides where we were able to spend time together hanging out with our band friends. This is about the only way a senior guy could talk to a sophomore girl. Todd asked me on a date to his senior prom (where he was voted King), and we ended up dating for three years. He taught me how to drive a stick shift pickup truck, and I taught him a few chords on the piano. We were best friends and inseparable.

We both grew up in loving homes with great families. Our parents taught us how to work hard, how marriages stay together, and the value of going to church. Neither of our families really talked about sex, money, politics, or religion all that much, but we both had wonderful loving homes.

Growing up, we both attended denominational

churches. We appreciated learning biblical foundational principles like baptism and forgiveness of sins, but to us it was just religion. Attending church was just a formality, as God didn't seem to interject into our daily lives. We both thought we were Christians, but neither of us had a personal relationship with Jesus. We went to church, but Jesus was not Lord over our lives. A good analogy might be that simply being parked in a garage doesn't make you a car. Similarly, us sitting in church pews did not make us Christ followers. It was not until later, once we both had a personal encounter with the Holy Spirit, when God taught us the difference between religion and relationship.

After we graduated from high school, we both realized we needed time apart to mature. Breaking our relationship off was difficult for me, but even more for my mother. She just adored Todd. My mom cried harder than I did about our breakup, but she said, "If it's meant to be, you will get back together." I knew there was truth in that statement somewhere.

Our parents had ingrained it into our heads that getting a college education was a must after high school, and so that is what we both did. Todd was a physics major with an education minor, and I was a music major studying vocal performance with a concentration in piano. I was career driven at eighteen years of age. I didn't want to get married or have children. I just wanted to sing and travel. Although neither one of us attended church in college, we would have said we were Christians. We thought we had the world by the tail and had all the answers, so there was no need for God. God was limiting, full of rules and regulations and that didn't look appealing. The college world was offering much better things, or so we thought. We both hit "rock bottom" in our early twenties. God was able to get our attention as life got to be a mess. He loved us both too much to leave us in our dark worlds with no Savior.

During my sophomore year, I developed performance anxiety, which made it difficult to justify pursuing my dream of singing in front of crowds of people. The constant negative critique from my music professors weighed on my self-esteem and I started to hate singing. I would avoid singing in front of my peers because my performance anxiety was so debilitating. I started taking an anti-depressant/anxiety medication to help control my fears, but it didn't do much for me. What was I going to do with my life if I couldn't perform music? I knew I was not called to be a music teacher for the public schools. Music was all I was good at. I couldn't think of anything else that I even wanted to change my major to, just to graduate with some kind of degree. I was losing my identity and I spiraled out of control.

I filled that year with drinking and going to parties with my music friends. All those things left me empty and lonely inside. In the quiet times, I knew something much bigger was missing in my life. I didn't have peace. I knew I needed direction, but I didn't know where to look for the answers. Nobody seemed to know which way I should head in my life, so when a college friend invited me to a nearby local church I agreed to go. I thought I would give God a try. Maybe He had the answers for me.

I started attending a college Bible study and became friends with so many great people. They talked about having a relationship with Jesus, being born again. I knew I didn't want more religion. They seemed to have peace and contentment, two things I didn't have in my life at the time. My stubborn, independent spirit was finally broken down, and I asked Jesus to be Lord over my life. It was the best decision I have ever made. I finally surrendered. Peace came over me, and I could finally relax about my unknown future. I knew God was walking with me now, and I didn't have to try and figure everything out. My purpose was to do His will in my life, not what my will was. I adopted the lyrics to the popular Carrie Underwood song as my own personal motto: "Jesus take the wheel." I was relieved to be in the passenger seat, along for the ride now.

Todd and I had completely lost touch with each other for a few years, but I "ran into" him at a softball game the summer he graduated college. He told me he accepted a job as a high school science teacher and was moving to Atlanta, Georgia. I told him I was happy for him, but I cried driving home that night after we said goodbye. Running into him brought back great memories of our high school days. I thought I would never see him again in my life, a realization which made me sad and lonely. It was then God showed me that I still had feelings for him.

DIVINE CONNECTION

I returned to college that fall not able to get Todd off my mind. I wondered how he was adjusting to his new life in Atlanta. Was he happy? I was sure he would have found a girlfriend down there. I wanted to call him and see how he was doing, but I didn't want to reach out to him if it wasn't what God wanted me to do. I needed to hear from God. I needed a "sign" that I was in God's will and not just following my own desires.

That is when I asked my college roommate, Kelly, to pick a number between one and ten. I told her if she picked my number, I would take that as a sign from God to go ahead and call Todd. If she didn't pick my number, I wasn't calling him. She picked the number three. I was shocked and fell back on my dorm bed in amazement. God had given me a crystal-clear sign. I told her Todd asked me to the prom April 3rd. That was my number! If Kelly had picked any other number, my destiny might have been completely altered. My faith was so encouraged as He spoke directly to me through Kelly.

Kelly had to trust me that the number three was

my number though. She said, "Karla, you would have said it was whatever number I picked!" It was my only regret. I should have written the number three on a piece of paper for proof because I would still have that piece of paper to this day as a reminder of God's faithfulness to me. It was my first of many specific encounters throughout my life that God was directing my path.

I finally got up the nerve and reached out to his mom because I didn't know his phone number in Atlanta. I still had his parents' phone number memorized from high school. I nervously called his mom. She sounded relieved that I was trying to reach Todd in Atlanta. She told me he could use a familiar, friendly voice from home as things were not going well in Atlanta. God knew what was going on. Todd needed some encouragement.

I was nervous calling him, but I knew God wanted me to reach out to him. He was happy to hear from me, and we agreed to get together when he was home for Christmas break a few weeks later. We met for a day of downhill skiing and talked about our lives. He shared with me that he was caught in a toxic environment. His personal life was full of lies and manipulation by the people around him. He was lonely, confused, and needing help to get out of the mess he was in. I think it helped him to share his story with me. I could listen with an objective perspective and fresh eyes. Something was very wrong, and it needed to end. God was getting Todd's attention. It was the turning point for Todd's faith walk.

We realized during our time together our friendship from high school was still there. We haven't been apart since. I guess the saying, "You don't know what you have until it is gone," was true. God had brought us back together. It was an answer to my prayer for direction in my life as well as Todd's and our parents'.

He gave his life to Christ that following spring. We were engaged in August and married four months later. I was a Christmas bride in 1997. When God moves, He sometimes moves fast. Todd's roommates from college thought I must be pregnant ... little did they know what was really happening.

BEGINNING

After our honeymoon, we immediately moved to Atlanta where Todd was teaching high school physics at Marietta High. He had bought a brand-new Mazda pickup truck with payments. We also financed a red Chevy convertible. Our thinking was, why not? Atlanta had beautiful weather for joy riding, and we had no children. Add those two payments to my student loans, and our debt story began. We walked into a life of financial slavery.

We were your typical broke newlyweds starting life out with a few wedding gifts. We were renting a tiny, one-bedroom apartment; our couch was a hand-me-down from four previous couples.

It had an ugly, orange-flowered slipcover and was propped up by college textbooks for the legs. For cheap entertainment we watched our fish swim around in their fifty-five-gallon tank while we watched free movies on TV. If we really felt like splurging, we rented a movie from the local Blockbuster movie rental store for two dollars. We were happy and living on love.

As young, born-again Christians just starting our faith walk with God, we had a lot to learn about God's kingdom, especially how money worked. We found a denominational church we both felt comfortable with that blended the traditional and contemporary services. Our church was in a very affluent area of Atlanta called Buckhead. It was the first time either of us was around people who drove Mercedes-Benzes to church and lived with gated driveways. We met people who loved the Lord and showed us southern hospitality. We saw extreme generosity. While we attended this church, God showed us that you didn't have to take a vow of poverty to be a Christian and that money was not evil. Money was a tool in God's kingdom to be a blessing to others. We saw genuine hearts in people who had the gift of giving and exuded joy when they operated in that gift. It sparked a desire in both of us to someday be a blessing to others in the kingdom of God with our resources.

We got involved with a Sunday school class for young married couples with the clever name, "No Hot Fudge, but We Have Great Sundays." This group became our family away from home. As newlyweds this church gave us a wonderful start to our faith and financial journey.

At our church I was able to open up a private piano studio, Karla's Keys, teaching thirty students. It was my first time running a business. I was making good money at fifty dollars an hour and thankful the church didn't charge me rent to use the piano and space. They viewed it as an outreach for their congregation.

I was also hired by the church's preschool to teach music to children ages two through five in the mornings. This schedule worked out well; I stayed at the church after preschool was over and taught piano lessons in the afternoon. Teaching toddler's music was not what I had pictured for my music career when I was taking all of those music performance classes in college, but I was happy to have a paycheck doing something with music.

On Sundays I played piano on the worship team during our church's contemporary service, and we both sang in the choir during the traditional service. We would give money in the offering basket as a "thank you" for letting me have a business at the church, but it wasn't a tithe. We never even thought much about the tithe. We thought the church was doing just fine without our small contribution. After all, we had a tight budget, and tithing was not included in our monthly expenses on a regular basis.

For the next two years any extra money we had

went to pay for Todd's graduate school. He was attending night classes at a local university and studying for a master's degree in information systems. This broad field of study also allowed him to potentially change careers if teaching turned out not to be his lifelong passion. We had to take out a few small loans through credit cards to pay for this degree. More debt. We were still in the daily grind trying to achieve financial peace through educational means to "hope" for a better paying job.

FIRST HOUSE

We would wonder how anybody could "get ahead" to save up for a down payment to purchase a house. To us, writing a rent check each month felt like "throwing money down the drain." Any financial advice we heard would encourage buying, not renting, and our rent payment was about the same as what a small mortgage payment would be. Creating equity in a house sounded wonderful. The banks at that time were also offering zero percent down on a home mortgage. Perfect! We didn't have any money to put down anyway.

Three years into our marriage we began talks with mortgage lenders to purchase our first house. We quickly found out that banks required three years of income tax returns to prove steady income. Todd had been a schoolteacher for three years and could supply tax returns, but I had just started my business as a piano teacher. We needed our joint income for a loan, but I didn't have three years of income tax returns to show the lender. My parents offered to co-sign with us. It was a formality to be approved for the thirty-year mortgage. Once we closed on the house, we removed my parents' names from the lien when we refinanced to a twenty-year loan. The co-signing was a blessing to us, but we probably could have waited another year and saved up for a larger down payment to avoid having to use my parents' names. Live and learn.

Our house was part of a new "cookie cutter" construction subdivision in a suburb of Atlanta. The construction company offered four house plans. Each style home averaged 1,400 square feet. They were small homes but perfect for two people with no kids. To add variety to the street, the builder required that no two houses of the same style be next to each other.

We were one of the first buyers in phase one of construction, so we were able to select our building lot and decide on which floor plan. We had first pick of both. This process started our love for custom homes. Who doesn't love to pick out everything? We were spoiled. It was like Christmas!

We chose a house plan with a vaulted ceiling, grey siding with black shutters, and a matching front door. Inside we selected oak kitchen cabinets and crème carpets. It was custom to us! We enjoyed watching our house being built. Each night after work we would go see the daily progress. One day we had a dirt yard, and the next day we had beautiful, rolled-out fresh sod. It was exciting to see our first home come together with our personal selections. We moved into our new house in the spring of 2000 with new debt.

Now, in addition to a mortgage payment and two car payments, we financed a beautiful baby grand piano. More debt. The piano payment wasn't huge, and we could afford it, so we bought it. The piano bench was the only piece of furniture we had to sit on in our downstairs living room. The orange, hand-me-down couch survived the move and was in our TV loft.

We were your typical, young married couple, just living life in debt and feeling good as long as all the bills were paid. We thought we were doing well financially, but we were actually in bondage. We were spending money as fast as it was coming in and living paycheck to paycheck.

OUR FIRST DOG

Now that we owned our own home, we could get a pet. We adopted our first dog Maxwell, a Wheaten Terrier mix, from a rescue shelter. We paid thirty dollars for him. His paperwork from the shelter said he had been found in a ditch, and that is all the history he came with. Max was a great dog. He loved to go for walks around the neighborhood. He would greet us each day when we came home from work by running completely around the outside of the house. We called it his "happy lap." At Christmastime when we flew home to New York, we bought a plane ticket for Max as well. It brought my mind peace to sit on the plane, look out my window below, and see Max being loaded onto the conveyer belt. He was easy to pick out in his blue crate with all the other luggage entering the cargo area of the plane. I was happy to connect with Max at the baggage claim in the Syracuse airport and see he was safe and sound from the flight. He was our "baby" for several years until we started our family. Little did I know how God was going to use our love for dogs to change our future financial path.

NEW LIFE SHIFT

In 2002 our daughter Mia was born. This is the season where every couple has to make the hard decision whether to have one parent stay home or both work outside the home. Our desire was for me to be a stay-at-home mom, but we were feeling the financial strain. We could not make the budget work without part of my income from the preschool or piano lessons contributing. I was thankful I could bring Mia to my part-time job at the preschool. They offered staff members free tuition for their children. This was a great opportunity for income while allowing me to be with Mia. Mia was in the preschool nursey, and I would walk by her nursery room and peek in the half door to see her sleeping in her swing. I had the best of both worlds, teaching music and being with Mia. We had found a way to balance income and a baby. (We thought we had all the answers … again.)

Each day when Todd was done teaching school at 2:45 p.m., we would meet halfway between the school where Todd worked and the preschool where I worked. Todd would take Mia home, while I returned to the church and taught piano lessons until early evening. This way we didn't need to pay for a babysitter. At times I was envious of my friends who had family close by for free babysitting, but we had no family to help us watch Mia. I was thankful Todd had a job that was done at 2:45 p.m. to be able to make that schedule work.

Todd would have dinner ready when I came in the door from teaching piano lessons, and Mia would be giggling in her highchair watching daddy cook the food. I loved watching Todd make silly faces at her. The time they shared together without me was laying a great foundation for their special bond they have now. We were both juggling jobs, taking care of Mia, and living paycheck to paycheck. We thought we were normal and didn't have any clue there was another way to live.

DREAM HOUSE

Atlanta was in a housing boom after the 1996 Olympic games. The economy was thriving, and suburbs were exploding with new construction. Everywhere you looked subdivisions upon subdivisions of beautiful custom homes were being constructed. On the weekends we would drive around and look through all the beautifully decorated spec homes going up and dream of one day owning a beautiful home like one of those. Our long-term plan was to stay in Atlanta, sell our small starter house, and upgrade to a larger one.

Each subdivision had a sign at the front of the entrance that would say, "Homes from the low $200s" or "Homes from the low $300s." Construction companies were building fast and making a lot of gorgeous homes. I would ask Todd, "Who's buying all these pricey homes? What do they do for a living?" We knew we were living paycheck to paycheck in our tiny home, so it was hard to imagine what a mortgage payment was on a house twice our square footage. We just didn't have peace about moving to a larger house.

Looking back on those years, we now realize people couldn't really afford the homes that were being built. Banks were lending money to people that would not typically qualify for a mortgage, and so were overextending homeowners. Greedy bankers and construction companies were pumping false air into the housing bubble until it finally burst in 2008, causing a huge recession in the economy.

A CHANGE IN OUR PLANS

We loved living in our tiny, 1,430-square-foot house in Kennesaw, Georgia, but after the tragedy of September 11th, 2001, we wanted to move home to upstate New York to be closer to family. We had enjoyed the custom building on our first starter home so much that we wanted to build again when we returned to our hometown. We began to look at blueprints to build our "dream home." We spent hours together pouring over house plan books, looking for that perfect house. It was fun dreaming of our growing family together living in our forever house. The anticipation of building a house was the focus of our life for quite a few months once we knew we wanted to move back to Upstate New York.

We decided on a 3,000-square-foot home with four bedrooms, two and a half baths, and cathedral ceilings. We wanted the master bedroom to be on the main floor in the event we couldn't climb stairs as we aged. We planned to stay in our dream home for the rest of our lives. We envisioned a separate piano room with crème carpet, able to absorb the sound from the baby grand. The piano room would have a French glass door so I could teach piano and check on my toddlers playing in the family room. Our kitchen was going to be custom built with a walk-in pantry. The great room would have a cathedral stack-stone fireplace and mantel with built-in bookcases on each side. Open shelving would define the bookcases throughout the house, along with ambient lighting for displaying special knickknacks. The upstairs bedrooms would open up to a loft with a handrail looking down into the great room. We also wanted an inground swimming pool in the future. Big dream. Big house. Big debt.

Due to the Atlanta housing boom, we were able to capitalize on the market and sell our house in three weeks. Short and sweet. After closing we had $30,000 in equity to put down on our dream home we wanted to build. That was the most money we had ever seen in our bank account. Having that much cash was also a taste of what being debt free was about. We look back now and wonder if the Holy Spirit was giving us a glimpse of what life should feel like? The dream house was starting to be reality.

We officially moved back to New York State in 2003 with cash in the bank and blueprints for our dream home. By this time I was pregnant with our second child, Carter. My parents' rental house became our temporary home while we built our house. Our cheap rent allowed us to save even more money towards our house construction, and we were happy to be living near family. We were looking forward to the free babysitting from our parents.

Todd found a job in Upstate New York, about an hour's drive from our hometown, as a technology trainer. Meanwhile I opened up another private piano studio, in addition to being offered a music minister position at the conservative denom-inational church we would be attending.

I was very excited about this music ministry opportunity because it was a way for me to use my musical gifts in a church and contribute to our monthly budget. We were adjusting to our new life living in New York and began scouting out property to purchase to build our home.

PREPARING

After driving around our county looking for land options, we found property just outside of town. This land was on a hill and had a beautiful view of the Black River Valley and the Adirondack Mountains, just what we were looking for. We learned an elderly couple who happened to attend our church owned the land. We took this coincidence as a sign from God and asked them if they would be interested in selling us four acres. They agreed to sell the land for $3500 an acre. We were amazed at their generous gift because $14,000 for four acres was significantly below market price. SOLD! We paid cash and were so thankful for the generous price. It was a God connection.

As we were clearing the property that fall in anticipation to build in the spring, we noticed the land had two small weeping willow trees the previous owners had planted down by the road. They were very small and blended in with all the goldenrod weeds we were mowing down. We decided to keep the sapling weeping willows and place our driveway between them. We could picture mature willows flanking our driveway entrance as they grew through the years. Not only would the willows make a beautiful entrance to our property, they would also have significance in the future financial plan God had for us.

Our winter was quiet because we were anticipating our second child Carter, who was born in February 2004. God blessed us with our dream family, a girl and a boy. I enjoyed being a stay-at-home mom with my babies. However, we were living out of boxes. We knew it was a temporary situation, but it was getting old. We had unpacked just enough kitchen items for me to cook a meal and a few toys for Mia to play with. We were making do with very little unpacked. It was time to build.

CHAPTER TWO

The Delusion of Debt

The rich rule over the poor, and the borrower is servant to the lender. Proverbs 22:7

During the month of March, we worked with our local bank to get our construction loan finalized. We were approved for a thirty-year mortgage with a large house payment, but we could afford it based on the information the bank was telling us. As long as we maintained both incomes, we could make the mortgage payment along with all our other payments. Our system of debt was still our way of life. It never occurred to us to ask God what His system was. We still thought debt was normal and our way of provision; after all, everybody else we knew in the church had mortgages and car payments.

We broke ground on our dream home in the spring of 2004. Since our previous experience of building a custom home in Atlanta had gone so well, we thought this building process would be just as much fun. Reality hit much harder this time around. Our home was not part of a large subdivision, like in Atlanta, where many subcontractors mass produce homes and keep the cost to a minimum. Here we had a single contractor.

The building contractor we selected had almost no experience building a house as the sole general contractor of a project. This was his first custom home with a building crew. We could tell he was nervous but up for the challenge. The two of us, as well as our contractor, were naïve on the building process, especially how the finances worked regarding a construction loan and a mortgage lender.

There are four main phases of a construction loan when you're building a house. Phase one is the foundation. Phase two is framing, siding, windows, and roof. Phase three is insulation, heating, plumbing, and sheetrock. And finally, phase four: kitchen cabinets, bathrooms, flooring, and paint. We assumed we'd receive a large amount of money up-front for our construction loan to begin building phase one. However, this was not the case. The mortgage lender did not release the construction "draws," or payments, until AFTER each phase of the house was completed.

In order to pass a phase, the building code inspector would inspect the work done in each phase and sign off on it before the bank would release the money. So, the only way to buy supplies for a phase before the lender would release the money was to use a line of credit at the building supply store. As the saying goes, we had to borrow from Peter to pay Paul.

Plans fail for lack of counsel, but with many advisers they succeed. Proverbs 15:22

THE STRESS BEGINS

Our general contractor began digging our basement, poured the foundation, and bought Styrofoam blocks for our basement walls on credit with the cement company. We were both completely oblivious to how the whole financial process worked with building a single custom home. This building process snowballed into a very stressful, complicated financial path we had to navigate with our contractor. He continued to place orders through a building supply company before he was paid … on credit. It was a balancing act to say the least.

For example, we could not receive the money for the windows until after they were installed and phase two was totally complete; however, the window company would not deliver $15,000 worth of windows with no payment first. The only way to pay for all the windows was through the contractor's line of credit. Eventually our contractor maxed out his line of credit, and we were forced to start using our personal credit cards to pay for building supplies. We were on a slippery debt slope, and our relationship with our contractor was deteriorating. We both were miserable.

Credit cards floated us financially for four months while we finished our dream home. When the contractor said he was ready to install the bathtub, I would run to a home improvement store and purchase it with our credit card. When the contractor needed all the light fixtures installed before the building code inspector came, we purchased them on credit cards.

Credit cards became our saving grace. Debt was accumulating faster than we could count it. Everything was costing more than we had budgeted with our contractor. Neither us nor our contractor had a good handle on the cost of materials, labor, or items for the house.

The financial stress was starting to show. One night while working on our house, in frustration from the financial pressure, Todd put his fist through our basement sheetrock! I had never witnessed this side of Todd's anger. Ever. I was shocked but also thankful we didn't need stitches at the emergency room. He was exasperated, his patience had run out, and he had hit his breaking point. It was a low time emotionally for us. We sat there, and I cried. We were tired of building and making decisions on the house. During this final push to complete the house, I remember thinking, "We can pay off all our credit cards we have accumulated when we get our phase four construction draw from our lender." It was the hope we needed to stay sane while we finished building.

COMPLETION

In December 2004 we were approved for an occupancy permit on our 3,300-square-foot dream home. We finished the whole process of building with a thirty-year fixed mortgage; however, we had racked up $25,000 on credit cards, in addition to owing our subcontractor for heating and plumbing. He was $11,000 over his original quote! (We found out later subcontractors bid low to receive the job but then typically go over their quote.) We were way over budget. Our debt was depressing, and we could feel the house becoming a curse and not a blessing. We didn't own the house. The house owned us. Nothing in our financial life matched what we were reading in the Bible.

"You will lend to many nations but will borrow from none. The Lord will make you the head, not the tail." Deuteronomy 28:12-13

We had the opposite of Deuteronomy 28:12-13. We were the tail and not the head, and we definitely had no money to lend to nations.

We didn't know how to solve the mess we were in financially. What was to be our beautiful dream home quickly became our Goliath nightmare; worse yet, we stuck our heads in the sand and ignored the problem by thinking this was "normal."

AND IT KEEPS COMING

Our first winter we had a reality check when we realized just how much propane it was going to take to heat a 3,300-square-foot house for the long New York winters. Our monthly propane bill was $500 a month, $300 over our original estimation with the banker. We had to use credit cards to pay for it. I can remember keeping the heat so low in our house to save on our propane bill that the kids and I would make forts out of sleeping bags on the living room floor and crawl underneath them to stay warm. I tried to make a game out of staying warm.

When we had company over, they kept their coats on because our house was not a comfortable temperature. One morning we woke up to our goldfish Jayjay floating dead in his tank because the water was so cold. We froze him to death. Poor little fish ... we had a funeral for him around the toilet bowl. To help heat the kitchen, I would leave the oven open after I had baked something so the hot air would help heat the room. Being cold was a miserable way to live. Being cold and broke was even worse.

Our second reality check came when we were fully assessed on the market value of our home the following year. Our assessment was $100,000 more than the bank originally quoted its value would be. This final assessment made our New York State property taxes for land and school ridiculous for our budget. They were far more than we had planned on. We were in house trouble. Our Goliath was getting bigger and bigger.

We knew something needed to change; do we sell this house we just built? What would our friends and family say? What would the town say? We didn't want to look like we had built a tower and without counting the cost.

"Suppose one of you wants to build a tower. Will he not first sit down and estimate the cost

to see if he has enough money to complete it? For if he lays the foundation and is not able to finish it, everyone who sees it will ridicule him, saying, 'This fellow began to build and was not able to finish.'" Luke 14:28-30

We had counted the cost with our banker, but we had not been given all the correct data to estimate the cost. We had too much pride to sell it and downsize so we just lived with our Goliath for four years, limping along in survival mode.

FINANCIAL RELIEF COMING

Todd took a new position as a school technology planner, which offered better pay. He liked the challenge of working with school districts and helping them develop their technology plans. The pay increase helped alleviate some of the monthly financial pressure but not much. I was a stay-at-home mom with two toddlers and babysitting three other children twice a week for extra money. I also was teaching private piano lessons in our home in the evenings to contribute to our budget.

Living paycheck to paycheck was normal those first years in our new house, and we felt the financial pressure every single day. It brought on depression and anxiety. When we had an unplanned expense come up, it went on the credit card. We thought the next month we would pay it off. However, the next month would roll around, and we didn't pay it off. If we were able to pay off the balance from the previous month, it wasn't long before we had another balance that was carried over. We were not living the abundant life. We were living with mediocrity.

REMEMBER MAX

When our son Carter was around the age of three, he put his hand in Max's dog dish. Max, in his old age, turned around and bit Carter on the lip. It started to bleed, and I knew then that we couldn't trust Maxwell with kids any longer. He was a grumpy old doggy. It was a hard decision, but we had to put him down. Driving him to the vet's office was the hardest thing I have ever had to do. I cried the whole way home.

We didn't get another pet for a few years after Max, because I was overwhelmed with the stage of life I was in. Potty training two toddlers, plus the three I was babysitting, was enough for me. I didn't want to potty train a puppy. We now had a few extra dollars each month because we didn't have to purchase dog food or have vet bills that we needed to pay for. God's timing was perfect. We missed Max but our lives were full of toddlers.

THE BURDEN GROWS, RISES TO THE SURFACE

We were both living in denial of how bad our financial situation was. Todd would be invited to meet guys for breakfast, and I would say, "We don't have any extra money for that." It wasn't fun to decline the offer, and he would get discouraged.

He wasn't feeling like an adequate provider, and I didn't like the way our financial situation was making him feel as a provider. As he worked long, hard hours and had an excellent salary, it was depressing to see the hopelessness he felt.

I knew we were living on the edge of a financial cliff, hanging on by our fingernails to avoid the rocky death below. I hated the feeling and knew we needed more income to have financial peace.

We thought about money all the time. The house had consumed our life. There were still things we needed to do on our property to have a fully functioning place. Our front yard still looked like a construction zone with no grass or landscaping … just mud. I would send the kids outside to play, and all they could do was make mud pies. They were always filthy, covered from head to toe in mud. I would use the garden hose to wash them off before they could come back inside the house. They thought it was fun, but to me it was just a lot of work.

We needed $400 for grass seed to put down the following spring on our enormous yard. We put it on our credit card. The first $100 worth of grass seed was washed away by a thunderstorm, and we had to replant. Wasted money. Nothing seemed easy. When the grass finally did come in, I mowed the yard with a push lawnmower. It was a miserable, all-day process to mow our large lawn with a push mower in the heat, but we couldn't afford a riding lawnmower.

Installing a wood burning fireplace in our house the following fall helped considerably to offset our propane bill. We knew we needed to buy the wood stove out of extreme necessity, but we went a few years with an unfinished hearth around the stove. We painted the plywood instead of spending thousands of dollars on stacked stone to finish it. (Just another sign of our survival mentality.) We burned twenty cords of firewood as a supplemental heat source. The heat and ambiance the fireplace gave off began to make our house feel like a home in the winter. We were starting to get a handle on our heating bill, but not in other areas of owning a home.

One hidden housing expense we never accounted for with our lender was the need to hire a person to come and plow our driveway in the winter. We didn't need a snow blower in Atlanta, and when we first rented in New York the farmer up the road came with his tractor to plow us out for free. Well, you can't live in northern New York without plowing your driveway almost daily in the winter.

Our first winter we realized it cost twenty dollars every time the plow man came. That quickly adds up when he was coming after each snow fall, sometimes three to four times a week. Our first plow bill was ridiculous and not in the budget. Todd called him and said, "Only come when we get eight or more inches of snow!" We needed to stop the bleeding of the wallet on our plow bill. It seemed more economical to purchase a riding lawn mower/snow blower tractor for our needs. We felt forced to buy a rider tractor which would save us money in the long run. The dealership was offering zero percent financing for three years. Perfect! We bought one. With debt.

ANOTHER PART-TIME JOB

When our children were old enough for public school, I saw an opportunity to earn extra money by being a substitute teacher in their school. I had my days free to be available if the school needed help. I was relieved when the phone would ring at 6:00 a.m. with the substitute caller wanting to know if I was available to come in that day. We needed the extra money, and I was always thankful for the call. It wasn't convenient to hang up the phone, jump in the shower, get two kids ready for school and all of us out the door in one hour, but we did that for years.

I was a regular face in the hallways at school. I enjoyed being in a classroom even though it was challenging to come into a classroom with twenty kids you don't know and try to teach. I was at least part of Mia's and Carter's worlds in elementary school, and I had a good pulse on the education they were receiving. I subbed three to four times a week, and the $750 a month I brought home was extremely helpful to our monthly budget.

We would get to the end of the month with me saying, "Well, looks like we can live here one more month." We were living in survival mode.

In 2007, my parents asked us if we would be interested in selling them two acres of our property so they could build a spec house on it to launch their custom home business. We were willing to sell two acres for $10,000 because the remaining two acres that our house and driveway sat on were more than enough. As we marked the new property lines, we kept all the beautiful trees on our acres to separate us from our new neighbors. It was a blessing to pay off a huge chunk of the construction credit card debt we had previously accumulated. Survival mode was at least getting bearable now.

POOL DRAMA

We were starting to understand that if we wanted a luxury item, like an inground swimming pool for our children, that we needed to save up and pay cash. I took a part-time job as an organist at a local denominational church on Sunday mornings. This church service didn't conflict with our own service that met on Sunday evenings, so this job worked well with our family. The church paid very well for the amount of time I was committing to, and I saved all my organ money for the pool. We budgeted a certain amount to spend on the pool; however, when the pool company started to dig in our backyard for the pool, they began to haul up trash buried underground. Trash! You have got to be kidding me. It was funny and not so funny at the same time.

The backhoe dug up old carpet, burnt wood,

two furnaces, bedsprings, and a bowling ball, to name a few items. We were all in shock. The pool company had never seen anything like it while digging for pools. We quickly realized the previous property owners had buried an apartment house that had burned down instead of paying to haul the house to the dump. Now the trash was our problem. Great. We were in another mess.

As you can imagine, paying to haul all this trash to the dump added a very unexpected, expensive cost to our pool. We were already over budget, and we didn't even have a pool yet! To make matters worse, the pool builders told us because we didn't have any virgin soil in which to place the foundation of the pool, they would have to recreate its bottom with cinderblocks, sand, and stone. This was a HUGE added price to the total cost, but what were we going to do with a huge hole in our backyard? We had to continue building the pool with credit cards because of the trash debacle. The use of credit cards was still our emergency fund, and having trash to remove was definitely an emergency cost.

We ended up with a gorgeous pool to enjoy with our children, but because of the costs we had incurred, we were thankful our local high school called about this time and offered me a full-time, nine-week maternity position as high school music teacher. Hallelujah! God was providing a way to pay for the extra pool expenses, and I enjoyed teaching choral music. Floating around in the paid-for swimming pool was a wonderful feeling. We were kind of getting the idea of living debt free.

THE STRUGGLE CONTINUES ...

We would hear people tell us to save money for our next vehicle, but we didn't have any extra money to set aside for future large purchases. Living paycheck to paycheck doesn't allow you to dream about saving money for the future. Hopelessness started to settle into our spirits. Todd would occasionally ask about our checking account, but I ran the daily checkbook and paid all the bills. He really had no idea what our expenses were for the month or how much I spent on groceries. I paid attention to every nickel and dime, so when Todd would want to eat out at a restaurant, I would have to say "No, we have no money." In disappointment he would say, "I make good money; where is it going?" I would reply in exasperation, "It takes a lot of money to live!" We really needed to sit down together and map out our budget for the month, but it would be years before we worked together on our money.

I can remember arriving on a family spring break vacation we were invited to in the Outer Banks of North Carolina with four dollars in our checking account. Four dollars. We had no emergency fund if we had an unexpected bill along the way on this trip. Wait--yes, we did! We had our credit cards if we needed to buy something. Why would you need an emergency fund when you had credit cards? Credit cards were the emergency backup plan.

Christmas shopping was stressful for years. Not only were we stressed about how to buy gifts for our children, but we hated the extra pressure we felt to buy gifts for extended family. When we had no extra money, it was difficult to have a giving spirit at Christmastime. We knew gifts were not the reason for the Christmas season, but we still felt pressure to give. When the kids wanted a "big girl and boy bedroom," I wrapped up throw pillows, comforters, and curtain rods for Christmas just so the kids had presents to open. How exciting for a four-year-old to open a curtain rod. We usually went into January before our Christmas debt was paid off. Bah humbug.

We had bought into the lie that we couldn't live without debt. To pay cash for everything was a pipe dream and not realistic. It takes a lot of money to pay cash for everything.

The truth was we didn't **believe** we could live without credit cards.

THE SCALES START TO FALL OFF ...

God used the movie Cinderella to teach me what is really going on in the economy today with what we **owe** versus what we **own**. It was a typical weekend night; we watched a lot of movies because it was cheap, indoor, winter fun with the kids. I was cuddled up on the couch with my children, microwave popcorn in the bowl, and a Diet Coke ready to enjoy. The kids usually picked the movie selection, and quite honestly, I didn't have a huge opinion on what we watched. I usually ended up falling asleep before the movie was done anyway, but this time I stayed awake with the musical version of this movie remake. I never dreamed God would use a classic story line to speak to me about our life. God can use anything to get our attention if we will listen.

Cinderella was a poor girl whose fairy godmother gave her a night out to attend the ball at the castle. Her fairy godmother provided her a ballgown and carriage to ride in for the evening. At the stroke of midnight, the beautiful, horse-drawn carriage turned back into a pumpkin, her horsemen back into mice, and her gorgeous ballgown back to rags. Her illusion was over, and it was back to reality. God showed me we live the same way; all our beautiful houses change into pup tents and our SUVs into rusted-out beater vehicles. That is all we own in reality. We say we "buy" things, when in reality we finance them. Thus, we trick ourselves into believing an illusion.

We lived this way seven long years. Delusion. We actually were helping pioneer a new church in our town, ironically called Abundant Life. Todd was the sound technician, and I was a worship leader. We were tithing when we felt like it, which was rare, and hoping for a financial miracle. Living in our Goliath. We might have been looking good on the outside, but we had no abundance on the inside. As they say in Texas, big hat no cattle.

CHAPTER THREE

Enough is Enough

The fear of the Lord is the beginning of knowledge, but fools despise wisdom and discipline.
Proverbs 1:7

W e needed to learn God's ways of handling money because our way was not working. We had gone around this mountain long enough. In fact, we had gone around the bottom of it so many times, we had carved a ditch in our stupidity. A popular definition of insanity is doing the same thing over and over hoping for a different result. We were stupid and insane. What were we doing wrong? We were making too much money to be this broke.

We finally cried out to God and prayed for answers. If you ask, He will answer you.

"Ask and it will be given to you; seek and you will find; knock and the door will be opened to you. For everyone who asks receives; he who seeks finds; and to him who knocks, the door will be opened." Matthew 7:7

God spoke to my weary, hopeless spirit and said, "Your provision is you. Not me. Your backup plan is debt. Your credit card is your idol."

Woah! I knew the Holy Spirit was convicting us. We needed to change our financial system and avoid debt. We were living like orphans, trying by our own strength to take care of ourselves and not allowing God to be our Provider. Our college diplomas were not solving the money problem as we were told in high school; we were living like the prodigal son.

"There was a man who had two sons. The younger one said to his father, 'Father, give me my share of the estate.' So he divided his property between them. Not long after that, the younger son got together all he had, set off for a distant country and there squandered his wealth in wild living. After he had spent everything, there was a severe famine in that whole country, and he began to be in need. So he went and hired himself out to a citizen of that country, who sent him to his fields to feed pigs. He longed to fill his stomach with the pods that the pigs were eating, but no one gave him anything.

"When he came to his senses, he said, 'How many of my father's hired men have food to spare, and here I am starving to death! I will set out and go back to my father and say to him: Father, I have sinned against heaven and against you. I am no longer worthy to be called your son; make me like one of your hired men. So, he got up and went to his father. But while he was still a long way off, his father saw him and

was filled with compassion for him; he ran to his son, threw his arms around him and kissed him. The son said to him, 'Father I have sinned against heaven and against you. I am no longer worthy to be called your son. 'But the father said to his servants, 'Quick! Bring the best robe and put it on him. Put a ring on his finger and sandals on his feet. Bring the fattened calf and kill it. Let's have a feast and celebrate. For this son of mine was dead and is alive again; he was lost and is found.' So, they began to celebrate."
Luke 15:11-24

We loved the phrase, "When he came to his senses," as we FINALLY were coming to our senses as well. Just like the prodigal son, we realized we had a "give me" attitude that was changing now through our circumstances to a "make me" spirit of humility. We humbled ourselves and asked God for forgiveness. Todd and I had lived long enough with lack and insufficiency, eating the pigs' slop, and doing things our own way. We didn't realize our identity through Jesus.

God was waiting for us to come home to a house full of abundance. We returned home like the prodigal son and accepted the robe and the ring. The robe of royalty in the kingdom of God and the ring of authority we have as children. We graciously *accepted* the *free invitation* to sit and eat at Father's table.

Jesus paid for the table. Jesus paid for the food. Jesus paid for the party. There is plenty for everybody who wants to accept the free invitation.

It was a long process to change systems and renew our minds to a new way of thinking. God's way of handling money is very different from the world's. It was going to be hard to switch kingdoms, but we were hungry for change. We realized we had the power to change our circumstances. We just had to choose.

Do not conform any longer to the pattern of this world, but be transformed by the renewing of your mind. Then you will be able to test and approve what God's will is--his good, pleasing and perfect will. Romans 12:2

THE CHANGE

First, we cut up our credit cards and went to a cash-only system. Wow. I didn't realize how hard it would be for me to cut them up. I felt I was chopping off an arm. Credit cards were our idol and we worshipped the financial peace we thought they brought us. Instead of relying on the Prince of Peace, Jesus, we had been living a life of deception. Credit cards offered us no peace; instead, they were a trap. They allowed us to say, "We'll pay them off next month." However, next month would roll around and we never paid off the previous month. It had been a way to stay in denial. Now we changed to debit cards to make online purchases only. Everything else was paid for in cash. Our bank offered an excellent fraud protection plan on our debit cards, so we were not worried about getting our bank account completely cleaned out. We couldn't live with fear. We had to trust God to protect our bank account.

I guide you in the way of wisdom and lead you along straight paths. When you walk, your steps will not be hampered; when you run, you will not stumble. Hold on to instruction, do not let it go; guard it well, for it is your life. Do not set foot on the path of the wicked or walk in the way of evil men. Avoid it, do not travel on it; turn from it and go on your way. Proverbs 4:11-15

The next month after we cut up our credit cards, Todd and I sat down together and looked over our monthly budget. We realized we were spending about $600 in miscellaneous items such as eating out, clothing, and entertainment. You gotta love that "miscellaneous" category. It's all the extra stuff you probably shouldn't be buying if you don't have the money to pay for it anyway. We had to rein it in.

We started to listen to the live on-air financial guru Dave Ramsey. Everything he said about debt made sense, and his message is based on the Word of God. It was the confirmation we needed to follow his "get out of debt" plan. Dave's plan is called the "Seven Baby Steps" to financial peace. Walking up the "Seven Baby Steps" gave us a guideline for our financial recovery and a track to run on. It was simple. We did not need a complicated financial plan. Below are the seven steps Dave Ramsey lists, adapted from his website:

Baby step one: save $1,000 in a starter emergency fund

Baby step two: pay off all debt (except the house) using the debt snowball

Baby step three: three-to-six months of expenses in a fully funded emergency fund

Baby step four: invest fifteen percent of our household income in retirement

Baby step five: save for college tuition

Baby step six: pay off your home early

Baby step seven: build wealth and give

We had cash envelopes for groceries and gas. No more eating out. Once we didn't have credit cards to fall back on, we felt really broke. We had no way to pay for an emergency, and I could feel anxiety rising up in my spirit. We quickly made it our first financial priority to get Dave's "baby step one" completed, which was a $1,000 emergency fund in the bank. We looked around our house and found a few things we could sell on the Internet to jumpstart our emergency fund. I had to say goodbye to my guitar, alto saxophone from high school, and rollerblades that were sitting dusty in our basement. We buckled down, got disciplined in our spending, and found the cash in our budget. Our small emergency fund brought us some much-needed financial peace.

Just like the Israelites leaving Egypt, once they crossed the Red Sea, they couldn't return. They had no option but to forge ahead with God's direction and spend some time walking in the wilderness learning how to follow God. We felt the same way with cutting up our credit cards. No turning back.

Over the next two years God provided our daily needs. Nothing fancy. Food and necessities. God was training us to hear His detailed instructions. We were like the Israelites after they crossed the Jordan River into the Promised Land. At that time they needed to hear God's detailed plan to conquer the territory. God's instructions can be very unusual, as they were in the case of the city of Jericho:

"March around the city once with all the armed men. Do this for six days. Have seven priests carry trumpets of rams' horn in front of the ark. On the seventh day, march around the city seven times, with the priests blowing the trumpets. When you hear them sound a long blast on the trumpets, have all the people give a loud shout; then the wall of the city will collapse and the people will go up, every man straight in." Joshua 6:3-5

The instructions God gave the Israelites were to march around the city seven times. Not two. Not six. Seven. Detailed plans. A unique strategy to get the victory. I'm sure there was mumbling as they walked the sixth lap, tired and hot from the heat, not seeing any results. Finally, on lap seven, with a shout, the walls fell in and they entered Jericho. Can you imagine their surprise when the walls just fell in front of their eyes? I'm sure there was an intense celebration!

We were now headed to our promised land as well. During our wilderness journey, cash was our only option, and we had to learn how to live within our means. The thought of paying cash for everything was daunting though. It takes A LOT of money to raise a family with cash. But cash was a great way to decide what we really needed versus what we wanted.

I shopped a few years at the Salvation Army store to purchase school clothes and seasonal items like winter coats. Both children needed expensive eyeglasses, and we wanted to provide our kids with good things like ballet and karate lessons. Using cash helped rein in our miscellaneous spending. When the cash was gone, we were done spending for the month. God was training us in discipline.

When I went shopping, I would ask myself, "Is this a want or a need?" It wasn't very often the item was a need. God was showing me His faithfulness every month. If I felt pressure to buy something that I couldn't pay cash for, I would walk away and say, "God I need You. You are more than enough for me. There isn't anything I need more than you."

It was a humbling time in our lives, but we both grew closer to God. He was now showing us His provision and faithfulness in our lives. We were being torn back down to the bare bones of what we needed to live so we could change our perspective and get our priorities corrected for what God was about to change in our lives.

FIRST THINGS FIRST

Todd and I were both on the same page and very committed to getting out of consumer debt. We believe our unity was a key to Todd's promotion. God saw our heart and blessed Todd with a new administrative position. Previously we would have enjoyed the increase in pay for personal expenses like eating out and shopping. But now we were convicted to start bringing our whole tithe to God, resulting in an increase in our giving. God was testing our hearts with our increase. Could we continue to be faithful with more income?

"Bring the whole tithe into the storehouse, that there may be food in my house. Test me in this," says the Lord Almighty, "and see if I will not throw open the floodgates of heaven and pour out so much blessing that you will not have room enough for it. I will prevent pests from devouring your crops, and the vines in your fields will not cast their fruit," says the Lord Almighty. Malachi 3:10-11

The Holy Spirit was taking us to "pruning school." We were convicted to bring the whole tithe, not because God was taking something from us, but because He was trying to get something to us. The tithe is a promise from God. The promise of protection over our children and property. The promise of abundance. The promise to bless the work of our hands. And the wakeup call that if you are not bringing the whole tithe, you are actually stealing from God. Ouch. Ouch.

We began to be cheerful givers. We understood that tithing was an act of worship and activated our faith. The tithe was our first line item in our budget, and everything else came after that. There were months when we were tempted to not tithe, but God always made a way. Sometimes we had to wait on buying something or fixing something. God was testing our heart. Could we be faithful with the increase? Did He still have our heart, or did money have our heart? God always received our first money, not the leftover.

The more you sow, the more you reap. It is a law in the kingdom of God. Sow corn. Get corn. Sow money. Get money. It is a cyclical pattern of give and receive, give and receive. Show yourself faithful and trustworthy, and you will receive more to manage.

> *Now he who supplies seed to the sower and bread for food will also supply and increase your store of seed and will enlarge the harvest of your righteousness. You will be made rich in every way so that you can be generous on every occasion.* 2 Corinthians 9:10-11

FINANCIAL AWAKENING

With Todd's new promotion and a very large tax return from the previous year, we were able to completely pay off our student loans. We were FINALLY done with baby step two. Our only remaining debt was the mortgage. The "debt snowball" Dave Ramsey describes was starting to roll in the right direction. The freed-up cash in our budget allowed us to quickly save up for a newer vehicle. We bought a Jeep Commander for $10,500 cash. I remember looking at the large stack of cash to purchase the Jeep and thought, "That is a lot of cash. CASH." We were paying for a vehicle with cash! Even the woman we bought the Jeep from wanted to meet us in a well-lit public area because we told her we were paying with cash, and she was nervous about receiving that much money.

We were now weird, and it felt wonderful. As Dave Ramsey says, "Live like no one else so later on you can live and give like no one else."

We decided to NEVER BORROW MONEY AGAIN.

EVER.

PERIOD.

Cash was the only way we were moving forward to purchase ANYTHING!

Even though we could have easily bought Todd a new truck with a payment from his new salary, we chose to stay debt free. Staff members at Todd's work would pick on his old truck. When he started it up and drove, a loose fan belt made a loud, squeaky sound. We could hear him pulling in the driveway way before the garage door went up.

Our kids were embarrassed to ride in Todd's truck to school because people would stare at our loud truck, but we were not ready to pay cash for a newer one. He didn't care what anybody thought of him. Todd drove that truck for several more years before we were able to pay cash for a newer one. We were debt free, except for our mortgage, and had cash in the bank for an emergency. There was nothing on this earth worth going back into bondage for. Once you are free, you are free indeed!

> *It is for freedom that Christ has set us free. Stand firm then, and do not let yourselves be burdened again by a yoke of slavery.*
> Galatians 5:1

We needed to watch our budget closely. We were keeping track of every dollar. I sometimes felt like a slave to the budget. I was constantly checking our budget making sure we were on track to not overspend. Todd and I would sit down every two weeks and go over each line item to stay connected to the plan. Money still consumed our lives, but we were growing, maturing, and getting the training we needed. It wasn't pleasant, but it was necessary. We were still migrating to the "promised land" of more than enough.

> *No discipline seems pleasant at the time, but painful. Later on, however, it produces a harvest of righteousness and peace for those who have been trained by it.* Hebrews 12:11

MINISTRY

From an early age our daughter Mia loved to dance. Everywhere we looked she was twirling. Even at McDonalds, as we were ordering our food, Mia was twirling. Twirling. Twirling. She never stopped.

She had a natural gift to dance so we put her in a local beginner ballet class at the age of six. She loved her beginner classes, and by fifth grade she was serious about her need for higher ballet training. Every little ballerina's dream is to go on pointe shoes. Ballet was not just a "fun" thing she wanted to do; she desired to be a professional ballet dancer. All I saw were dollar signs. I knew ballet was expensive. Training was expensive, and pointe shoes are $100/pair.

We attended a performance by a professional Christian ballet company called "Light of the World Ballet" and knew this was where Mia needed to train for the next level. God was showing us an opportunity for Mia to use her gift of dance for the kingdom of God. However, the ballet company was not local.

The ballet school was an hour and a half drive each way to Syracuse, New York (three hours in the car a day), and the higher technique classes she needed met three days a week. Moving to a different ballet studio was a serious decision. It was a huge time and financial commitment for us, but the exceptional ballet instruction and biblical teaching was worth the commute. It seemed overwhelming to carry the weight of all the driving by myself. I was ready to commit, regardless of other families joining me, because I knew Mia needed the higher ballet training. I reached out to another ballet mom to see if they would be interested in joining us at the Light of the World Ballet school. They agreed it was a great opportunity for our ballerinas to learn Christian dance ministry together and share the long commute. Within a few days, God brought two more families to join our carpool. I was so thankful God brought divine ballet connections. The Lord was clearly showing us Mia's path for her life, and we were able to afford the training. We traveled and trained with Light of the World ballet for eight years. The discipleship she received there changed her life. It was worth every penny and hour we spent in the car commuting.

Our kids were learning to ask a month in advance if they needed new pricey ballet pointe shoes or new lacrosse equipment because everything went in the budget. We had large ballet tuitions, a lot of expensive soft contacts to buy with four people, sports equipment, and truck repairs so we could pass inspection. We were juggling the budget month to month. Every dollar had a name.

We still thought about money all the time. Is that in the budget? Did we spend all our "eating out" money this month? In our minds we were still in slavery. We had to keep close records of each little place we were spending money. It was eye opening how much the little things added up. A fancy latte coffee here, new ballet tights there. A birthday present here and a movie ticket there. The little purchases can destroy a budget. We were learning to pay attention to where each dollar was going.

Catch for us the foxes, the little foxes that ruin the vineyards. Song of Solomon 2:15

As we thought about everything we needed to pay for with cash, our poverty mindset started to talk to us, and fear set in. We would think to ourselves:

"How are we going to pay for a new pickup truck with cash? They are expensive."

"How are we going to pay for two college educations? Tuition is outrageous."

"We will never be able to afford to travel with kids -- Have you seen the price of airline flights for four people?"

"It takes a lot of money for a wedding."

Our heads were filled with thoughts of fear and dread for the future. We were starting to feel stressed about how to pay for it all without going back into debt! There is only so much time in the day for a second job. Or a third part-time job. We just couldn't run that fast. There are just a few hours in the afternoon each day to teach piano lessons. We were maxed out and had no more ideas on how to create more income. A paycheck can only be spread around so much. It was overwhelming to think about how much everything cost. Sometimes we wanted to just go back and sit in our ignorance. It was easy to start to complain like the Israelites did to Moses coming out of bondage in Egypt.

> *The whole Israelite community set out from Elim and came to the Desert of Sin, which is between Elim and Sinai, on the fifteenth day of the second month after they had come out of Egypt. In the desert the whole community grumbled against Moses and Aaron. The Israelites said to them, "If only we had died by the Lord's hand in Egypt! There we sat around pots of meat and ate all the food we wanted, but you have brought us out into this desert to starve this entire assembly to death."*
> Exodus 16:1-3

Sometimes Egypt looked easier. Sometimes it looked easier to just have a credit card and sit and eat the food in bondage. But we knew we were called to live free. We wanted to live in our promised land with more than enough just like the Israelites. We knew God would take care of us now, but the process seemed slow and painful.

DIVINE PROGRAM

One day while flipping through television channels, I came across a Christian program on Daystar, *Fixing the Money Thing*. The pastors, Gary and Drenda Keesee, were talking about biblical finances. Something triggered in my spirit, "You need to listen to this program." I stopped cleaning the house and sat down to listen. God used this program to get my attention. We were about to have a God "download" that would forever change our lives.

Pastor Gary was talking about God's way of handling money through *revelation*. He was talking about how God has no money in heaven, but He knows all things that pertain to life. God knows where and how to create money in the marketplace because nothing is hidden from Him. God has the answers.

I was intrigued. Everything the pastor said made sense. It was truth. I knew it. We needed help to fix the money thing for our future. He was preaching from the Scriptures in 2 Kings 4:1-7, and I found myself relating to the story.

The wife of a man from the company of the prophets cried out to Elisha, "Your servant my husband is dead, and you know that he revered the Lord. But now his creditor is coming to take my two boys as his slaves."

Elisha replied to her, "How can I help you? Tell me, what do you have in your house?"

"Your servant has nothing there at all," she said, "except a little oil."

Elisha said, "Go around and ask all your neighbors for empty jars. Don't ask for just a few. Then go inside and shut the door behind you and your sons. Pour oil into all the jars, and as each is filled put it to one side."

She left him and afterward shut the door behind her and her sons. They brought the jars to her and she kept pouring. When all the jars were full, she said to her son, "Bring me another one."

But he replied, "There is not a jar left." Then the oil stopped flowing.

She went and told the man of God and he said, "Go, sell the oil and pay your debts. You and your sons can live on what is left."

After reading this story I was so encouraged. I believed God could help us just like He helped the widow. She was a child of God just as much as I was. She asked for help from the prophet and so could I. We are not here on this earth alone to fend for ourselves. The prophet didn't give her a handout for the day but changed her financial future completely. What a revelation!

She was fearful that she would lose her children because she couldn't pay off her debt. Can you imagine what our world would be like if the lender could come take our children? Our society would be a lot slower to use debt.

God gave her a divine strategy to pay off her debt with a specific plan: jars of oil. She listened to the unusual, home-based business plan and walked out the specific steps with her kids. She asked her neighbors for empty jars. I'm sure she was wondering how they were going to be filled with oil in her house. She didn't care what people thought of her; she was going to do what the prophet told her to do.

She closed the door to her house behind her children. I believe she was told to close the door so she wouldn't get distracted from her assignment and would ignore all the people who were asking her why she was collecting all the jars in the town. Gossip can be a dream killer. Sometimes things need to stay private behind closed doors when you have a divine strategy so the enemy doesn't pick up on the plan of God.

She obeyed the specific instructions and started pouring oil into her empty jars. Only when her kids brought all the jars and there wasn't another jar in her town did the oil stop flowing.

She sold her oil in the marketplace, paid off her debt, AND had more than enough to live on the rest. God made a way for her and her children to be well taken care of for the rest of her days. Amazing story! She followed instructions, received the provision, and never looked back.

It was time for me to ask God where my oil was.

CHAPTER FOUR

His Plan

"For I know the plans I have for you ... plans to prosper you and not to harm you, plans to give you a hope and a future." Jeremiah 29:11

One spring morning in 2012, after I put my kids on the school bus, I sat down on my front porch to enjoy my gorgeous view of the valley and talk with God. This was my normal quiet time with God, and I loved stopping from my busy morning schedule to seek God's face. I remember sipping my hot coffee and asked God out loud with great anticipation, "Where is my oil?"

"What can I do in my house?"

"How are we going to live debt free from here on out?"

"I don't have anything in my house except for a few dollars."

"Show me where my oil is. I need the PLAN!"

I really wasn't sure I would get an immediate reply to my questions, but I was desperate for our answer. I knew He would answer me eventually. My faith was connected to the Word of God just like the widow asking the prophet for her answer.

I knew He had a plan for me as well. I was going to be content and wait patiently for His answer because I didn't have a clue what could possibly be in my house. I was ready to wait a month or a year or a few years, but within minutes deep in my spirit I heard my answer.

"You can do puppies."

I knew instantly He was referring to goldendoodle puppies. Over the years I would watch my mom deliver puppies when her goldendoodle mamas were in labor, and I would help her with bath time when it was time for her puppies to go home. It was something I was familiar with but didn't see myself breeding puppies, and we currently didn't live with a dog.

The conversation continued...

I asked the Lord, "How many am I supposed to get (goldendoodles)?"

He answered, "How many children do you have?"

"I have two children."

"Start with two puppies."

I was elated to have heard THE PLAN for me. A peace washed over me. I had never thought about breeding puppies. It was revelation to me. It was a word of knowledge from God, and I knew which direction to go.

I knew how much work went into potty training a puppy, both from having Maxwell and a litter of puppies at my mom's house, but I KNEW I had heard from God. Puppies were our answer. This idea didn't come from me but deep inside my spirit. Puppies were going to be our "jars" of oil.

WHAT IS A GOLDENDOODLE?

A goldendoodle puppy is created when a purebred golden retriever is bred with a purebred standard poodle. The first generation goldendoodle was created to be a hypoallergenic dog, using the poodle for curly hair that sheds less and the family friendly personality of a golden retriever. The goldendoodle is very popular for these traits. However, the first-generation puppies were still shedding too much hair, so the second-generation goldendoodle, called F1b, was created. This F1b breed is considered hypoallergenic with minimal shedding, making it desirable for people with allergies to have a family dog as a pet. There is high demand in the marketplace for a "doodle" that has these specific traits, and God knew that.

SHARING THE PLAN

I couldn't wait until Todd was home from work that evening to share with him my good news. When Todd walked in the door, I told him to sit down because what I was about to share with him was going to be a HUGE download of divine information.

I shared my conversation that God and I had

together earlier that morning. I shared that we were to partner with God for a goldendoodle, home-based business. I explained that our new "oil," goldendoodle puppies, would be funding my assignment as a mom and our kids' college education. This new income would also allow me to scale back my piano studio, which was after school hours, and concentrate on our children's afterschool activities. Our children needed me to be available to drive ballet carpool and attend soccer games. I loved being involved in my children's lives. They were our number one priority.

The plan was for me to raise goldendoodle puppies for market, but it would be up to God to make puppies. I knew this business wasn't my idea, and I certainly can't make puppies. It was a divine strategy. Puppy provision!

Todd's one-word response was, "Really?"

He was in shock. It was a lot of information to process all at once.

After he absorbed the unusual plan, he was 100% on board. I was so thankful he confirmed God's plan with me. We were in unity. We could both pull together. Puppies were our answer.

> *Two are better than one, because they have a good return for their work: If one falls down, his friend can help him up.* Ecclesiastes 4:9-10

We told the kids what our family business plan was from God. We knew we needed the whole family to be supportive to pull this business off in our home. We told our kids they were going to be helping and not complaining as we worked on the business. Our kids were in elementary school and very excited they were each getting a puppy.

"Any kingdom divided against itself will be ruined, and a house divided against itself will fall." Luke 11:17

I called my mom who was breeding goldendoodle puppies at that time. I asked her if she minded if we also started breeding puppies for our college funds. She agreed it would be a good idea. I was relieved we had her blessing on our business. (She didn't know the back story of the previous conversation I had had with God.) God used my mom's blessing to confirm His plan for us. I didn't want any competition or strife between my parents and us. I knew we had our plan, and God was our partner. We agreed to purchase two puppies from her summer litters in 2012.

HIDDEN TREASURE

We were taking a leap of faith to buy goldendoodles to breed. At that time the market price for a goldendoodle puppy was $1,200 per puppy. We did not have the money to buy one goldendoodle, let alone TWO. We were WAY outside our comfort zone. We would never purchase such expensive dogs for our family as pets. What if we haven't heard from God? What if we take the financial risk and our goldendoodles can't get pregnant? We were not really interested in wasting money, but

I KNEW I had heard from God. He had the plan, and we were to walk it out in obedience. We proceeded with fear and trembling.

"The kingdom of heaven is like treasure hidden in a field. When a man found it, he hid it again, and then in his joy went and sold all he had and bought that field." Matthew 13:44

God had shown us where the treasure was. The treasure was inside His creation. God knew where the secrets were hidden just as He demonstrated in the story of the widow with the oil. We needed to get our "jars," and God would fill them with puppies. We were not going to be disobedient now and ignore the plan. Purchasing two goldendoodle puppies was a business investment for us, and it was scary to step out, but we had to sow seed to get a harvest.

BELLA AND GRACIE

My mom was gracious and gave us a family discount. For us each puppy cost $800. We were appreciative of the gracious discount but still needed to come up with $1,600. That was a lot of money to us. We worked each month to save approximately $250 towards the purchase price while we waited for our goldendoodle puppies to be born.

We had a garage sale to create extra money to put towards buying our doodles. The kids sold toys. I sold Christmas decorations and clothes. Todd went through the basement and found leftover floor tile from building the house. If we didn't have any immediate need for something, we sold it. We wanted to buy our fields.

SHUTTING "THE DOOR"

When we shared our plan with some of our friends and family members, we were laughed at. They thought we were crazy getting two dogs.

"They're expensive."

"You'll have large vet bills."

"You can't make any money selling puppies."

"They'll tie you down to your house."

It was all so discouraging to hear. We were willing to get criticized from those closest to our lives. It wasn't easy not having family support, but we were not interested in what our family wanted us to do. We wanted to do what God's plan was for us. We shut the door, just like the widow with the oil, and got busy raising our "jars" and ignoring the distractions.

Our first two puppies, Bella and Gracie, came to live with us the fall of 2012. Bella was a chocolate-colored goldendoodle while Gracie was crème. They were from two different litters but shared the same stud (dad).

Our lifestyle had to change to accommodate two puppies. We had to "puppy proof" our house. Legos had to be put away, and Barbie doll shoes needed to be picked up off the floor. We installed an inground fence around our house. We bought collars and name tags. We had to potty train two puppies, twice the work. Having two puppies pee on your carpet wasn't easy.

There were many days I would get discouraged and think, "What are we doing?" and Todd would say, "What did GOD say?" I knew we were in this for the long haul. We were not quitting. We needed perseverance to push through those few training months.

Other professional breeders recommended to wait and breed for puppies on the second heat cycle. This means that you do not breed on the first heat. The first heat cycle occurs when a dog is around one year of age. I must admit it was quite gross to have blood on my floor. I mopped my floors every day for the fourteen-day heat cycle. I also watched my yard for neighborhood males who wanted to make a litter of puppies. We did not need the wrong kind of puppies. We needed to be vigilant and guard our flock.

The second heat cycle occurs around six months to a year beyond the first cycle. So, the startup time to breed for puppies is at least a year and a half. Time. Patience. Perseverance. There was a gestational period to even launch a puppy business. So, I stood on Galatians 6:9 many, many times and said it out loud:

And let us not be weary in well doing: for in due season we shall reap, if we faint not. (KJV)

It didn't take long to have this verse memorized. I said it ALL. THE. TIME. It seemed every day we were faced with challenges from living with two dogs, but this verse reminded my weary spirit that there was a reward coming. God does not give you a task and not give you the reward. He is a good Father!

I could feel hope and financial peace rising in my spirit. This strategy in the marketplace was going to be our answer to fix the money thing. If we had two litters of puppies (eight pups in each litter) and sell them at $1,200 each, the gross profit would be $19,200. That would certainly go a long way to help our monthly budget and live on cash for our future. "Cash is king," as Dave Ramsey often says in the opening lines of his radio program.

WILLOWGREEN GOLENDOODLES

During the two years we were raising Bella and Gracie, we prepared our home and came up with a business name. It seemed natural to use the willow trees on our property and our last name of Green to create our business name: "Willowgreen Goldendoodles."

Todd bought the domain name willowgreen-goldendoodles.com on the web and launched our webpage to promote our future puppies coming in 2014. We also created a Willowgreen Facebook page and linked that to our home webpage. Social media was free advertisement which was helpful to maintain a low startup cost for our business.

God was using Todd's background in information systems to create the technical side to running a business, which I knew nothing about. We made a great team.

We had to hire a new tax professional to teach us how to work through starting a new home-based business. We were clueless. We had to open a DBA (doing business as) at the county courthouse, open a business checking account, and start saving all our recipes for tax purposes. Starting a new business required us to be stretched. We needed to learn a lot to run a home-based business. Our tax advisor showed us there are many benefits to operating a home-based business.

We had to shop differently. Dog food, dog shampoo, and vet bills were all part of our business expenses. I had to separate my items at the stores and check out twice. Our personal items were rung up separately from the business expenses. I always had both debit cards with me and both checkbooks, personal and business. Part of heating our home and part of our phone bill was now a tax write off.

The integrity of the upright guides them, but the unfaithful are destroyed by their duplicity.
Proverbs 11:3

The business resulted in a financial loss our first two years of operation. We had Willowgreen expenses, but no puppies to show for a profit. However, we wanted to be established as a serious business before our harvest came in. We also wanted to run our business with extreme integrity because, after all, only God could bless our business. We were going to report all income, pay our taxes, and tithe. We were not foolish to think that God couldn't see what was going on behind closed doors. Nothing is hidden from God. We knew God would not partner with mediocrity. His name was also on the line. He wants to shine brightly in a dark world.

Our third year we had to show Willowgreen Goldendoodles was profitable through our taxes, or we would be considered a hobby to the government. We were walking in faith that God would do what He said He would do. Only He could make our business successful. We needed divine puppies.

We remodeled part of our basement to be used for whelping, or birthing, puppies. Todd made a fifteen-by-fifteen-foot puppy nursery room which was large enough to hold two litters at the same time. Both whelping pens were separated by a twenty-four-inch wall which we could climb over, but which keeps the mamas separated and puppies safe in their pen. For easy cleaning and disinfecting, we installed white board around the bottom wall of each whelping pen.

Using leftover paint from building our house, we decorated the walls with a landscape portrait showing blue sky, green grass, a few brown trees, and a huge yellow sun in the corner. We used the kids' handprints for adorable, colored leaves on the trees and flowers. They had fun painting their hands and pressing them up against the wall. It gave the room a cute personal touch. We made it a fun family art project to enjoy together.

Our family enjoyed the process of prepping for puppies. Just like the widow in 2 Kings 4, we had closed the door to our house and used our kids to help us prepare to start pouring into our "jars."

It wasn't always easy and enjoyable having two puppies to keep track of. Normally we let the doodles outside to run and potty on the grass in the inground fenced area. The first few months, as puppies, they were very good about staying in the fenced area. We could trust them to stay in the yard without watching them every minute.

THE THIEF CAME

One dark, snowy winter night when the puppies were five months old, I arrived home late after a women's meeting and noticed our doodles were not in the driveway. They usually were there to greet me. I knew instantly something was wrong. I went in the house hoping they were inside. They weren't. They had run through the fence. The snow was so deep they didn't feel the electric shock. We all started to panic.

We started calling their names. They didn't come. We got in both vehicles and drove up and down the road looking for them. We ran through the snow to the neighbor's house yelling and screaming their names. I was so fearful they would be hit by a car, or worse, a snowplow. I didn't think they could survive the night outside if they were lost. It was going to be below zero during the night, too cold for puppies to make it without finding shelter. I was crying. I was so stressed, and fear was overtaking my thoughts. We needed to fight in the spirit.

Prayer was our only answer. We started praying for their protection and safe return to us. They were our provision. We prayed as a family, agreeing together that God knew where they were, and He would bring them home. We stood on the Word of God and spoke scriptures out loud. We stood on the promise of the tithe, that God would rebuke the devourer. Our enemy wanted nothing more than to kill, steal, and destroy Bella and Gracie, but we declared our enemy, Satan, had no authority to steal, kill, or destroy them. They were protected. Hands off!

In our midnight hour, literally...midnight, we learned as a family how to fight in the supernatural. God was fighting this battle for us, but we were releasing our faith.

After several hours of searching in the dark we decided to leave the light on and try to sleep. It was now a waiting game. I went to bed crying. I was so upset. We loved our doodles as pets and wanted them home safe, but I also saw our business closing before we ever had a litter of puppies to sell. It was around 1:00 a.m. when I thought I heard paw scratches on the front door. I got up and went to check on the front door. I was so happy to see BOTH of them at the front door. They were cold and tired but home together safe and sound. We praised God and thanked Him for watching over them.

Our kids saw firsthand the power of prayer and standing on the word of God. Our whole family's faith was so encouraged that night. We were all learning how to speak out loud and stand on God's promises.

The next morning when it was light outside, we were able to see exactly where they had crossed the line and were able to follow their snow tracks into town where they had chased a wild bunny.

We had a new problem then as the inground fence really wasn't keeping them inside our yard with the large snow drifts. Every few months they would be gone chasing something. They didn't mind taking the electric zap for deer, woodchucks, skunks, or bunnies. We had plenty of wildlife for chasing. Every time they would be gone, I would pray and ask God to protect our "jars." It was always stressful when they ran away from home. I didn't know if they would get lost or hit by a car. I had to really surrender this part of the business to God and trust Him that He was watching over our doodles. They always came home. Sometimes, though, they came home smelling like a skunk, which required a lot of work bathing them to get the smell out of our house.

Do not be weary in well doing.

FIRST BREEDING

In the spring of 2014 both our doodles came into heat together, and we bred them with my brother's stud, Tucker. A dog's pregnancy gestation is sixty-four days so we had a few months to wait in anticipation for our puppies to arrive. We were so excited to finally be having puppies after two years of waiting! We talked with our children about having puppies coming and what we would be doing together to take care of them. We worked together prepping the whelping pens, but around day fifty neither mama doodle was looking pregnant. I couldn't believe it. I was so discouraged. My faith was turned upside down. We did not have puppies coming from either doodle. What? This can't be. I had to fight the negative thoughts in my head saying, "Ha! you didn't hear from God."

This is where our faith was tested. Did we miss God? Maybe we didn't hear the plan? Why would He tell us to start breeding and then both doodles not get pregnant? It just did not make sense to me. We wondered if we should quit on the business and not try to breed again. We needed encouragement. We needed to hear from God. What were we supposed to do now?

We found our answer in Luke 5:1-7:

One day as Jesus was standing by the lake of Gennesaret, with the people crowding around him and listening to the word of God, he saw at the water's edge two boats, left there by the fishermen, who were washing their nets. He got into one of the boats, the one belonging to Simon, and asked him to put out a little from shore. Then he sat down and taught the people from the boat. When he had finished speaking, he said to Simon, "Put out into deep water, and let down the nets for a catch."

Simon answered, "Master, we've worked hard all night and haven't caught anything. But because you say so, I will let down the nets." When they had done so, they caught such a large number of fish that their nets began to break. So they signaled their partners in the other boat to come and help them, and they came and filled both boats so full that they began to sink."

So, what did Jesus tell the fishermen to do after they worked hard all night and caught no harvest? Fish again. What did God tell us to do? Fish again. Our circumstances did not look like God was coming through on His end of the business, but we stood on what He had told us to do. We were to persevere. We launched out into the deep and prepared to fish again.

We waited patiently another six months before our doodles had another heat cycle and decided to try a different stud the next time. It just didn't make sense that both goldendoodles didn't have puppies. We were hoping that Tucker was the problem, not our doodles. We contacted a local labradoodle breeder and asked if she had a stud we could hire. She did, and we bred both Bella and Gracie again with a different poodle stud named Prince. During the sixty-four-day gestation I would speak Deuteronomy 28:4 out loud to strengthen my faith with the Word of God. I would start speaking the verse as it was written: "The fruit of your womb will be blessed, and the crops of your land and the young of your livestock- the calves of your herd, and the lambs of your flock." And then I would add for my specific situation, "and the puppies of my dogs." I figured goldendoodles and lambs were in the same four-legged, curly category, and I wanted to cover all my bases.

SECOND BREEDING

After sixty-three days this time, both of our doodles looked pregnant. We were excited about puppies finally coming. We prepped the whelping pens with blankets, towels, a nose sucker, scissors, and string. I would bring Bella and Gracie down to acclimate them to the whelping pens. I was hoping to be in charge of where we would like them to deliver puppies. I was very naïve to the whelping process. Humans do not tell a dog where to have puppies.

Finally, we were in labor! Gracie began to "nest" in my bedroom closet. She would scratch the floor and circle the ground for her spot. I didn't want puppies to come in my closet. However, when a puppy is finally coming out you really don't have a say where and when. I shifted all my dress clothes and high heels over to the side of my closet to make a whelping area. Gracie delivered her puppies on my closet floor. Karla was in control of NOTHING. My type "A" personality as a perfectionist and planner went right out the window.

THE FIRST DROP OF OIL

The first puppy came out in a perfect "sac." Gracie's natural instincts kicked in and she broke open the sac and chewed the umbilical cord off. I know, TMI. I didn't have much to do except sit in amazement and watch the harvest arrive. I did like to dry off each puppy with a towel, check the puppy's health, and rub their little chests to get all the fluid out of their lungs. But for the most part, nature knows what to do. It was a miracle.

After she was done laboring, I moved her downstairs to the whelping pen with her puppies and shampooed my closet rug. It was a small price to pay for a litter of healthy puppies.

Do not be weary in well doing.

We delivered thirteen puppies between our first two litters. We had waited two years, but we finally had a harvest. Praise God!

CHAPTER FIVE

Oodles of Doodles

The fruit of your womb will be blessed, and the crops of your land and the young of your livestock—the calves of your herds and the lambs of your flocks. Deuteronomy 28:4

Bella had six beautiful F1b goldendoodle pups, and Gracie had seven. Our doodles could get pregnant! We found out from our veterinarian that the first stud we had tried to breed them with was too old. The joy of knowing we had two healthy doodles that could have puppies was fantastic news. We did have "empty jars" to pour and fill. I was so thankful we had "fished again" and didn't give up on the first failed attempt.

After our puppies were born, we immediately placed individually-colored collars on each puppy so we could distinguish between them. No two puppies had the same collar, and they wore their special colored collar the entire time with us. I usually picked red, orange, yellow, pink, and purple collars for females and blue, green, gold, and silver for the males. I was surprised to learn a lot of children would select their puppy based on which collar color they liked. I even had two families name their puppies "Bleu" because both of their puppies had worn a blue collar.

Once they had collars on, we took a newborn photo of each pup in our puppy photo booth. The photos were then uploaded to our website where families could view and select which puppy they wanted to adopt. We would describe the gender, color of each puppy, and the collar color it was wearing under its photo. For example, a puppy description might read as such: "Caramel Female Yellow Wave Collar" or "Chocolate Male Green Collar."

We advertised our puppies in an Albany, New York, newspaper and a Westchester County newspaper outside of New York City for $1,200 per puppy. We paid a few hundred dollars in advertisement fees to submit our ads, but it was well worth it to get exposure to the greater Albany and New York City areas. Our target families who could afford a goldendoodle puppy would be closer to both of these cities. I was a little nervous spending that money, but I knew we had to spend money to make money, and it was also a business expense. We needed to sow into our business to get it off the ground. I was hoping to sell one puppy through the two ads and recoup my costs. A one-time ad placed in the right city, with God bringing the buyers.

Our ad stated we had F1b goldendoodle puppies available and to visit our website willowgreengoldendoodles.com to view the pups available. Families would select their puppy from the newborn photos and submit their deposit to reserve a pup.

HOPE RISING

When our first $300 deposit check arrived in our mailbox from a family in New York City, I started to cry. I was so thankful for the hope this business was bringing us. People were sending us money! Reality was setting in. This was a REAL business. This was REAL money coming in. Praise God! I could feel my spirit rising and hope flooded into my heart. We had a business that could make a profit. A niche in the marketplace. Our jars were filling up and we were going to market.

After all the deposit money arrived, I paid the stud owner two stud fees of $600 each. It was a business expense but worth every penny.

POURING PUPPIES

We enjoyed having our little goldendoodle puppies in our nursery downstairs. We left the basement door open at all times so our mamas could be upstairs with us but could nurse their puppies at any time. Our kids loved to cuddle them.

As each puppy was adopted, we would start calling each puppy by the name the owners had selected. It was fun to hear all the names of each puppy. Our very first puppy's name was Max Lemon (you could tell when a child was naming a puppy, as they were strange and unusual names). We had other names: Porter, Oscar, Stella, Remi,

Willow, Zola, Jake, Pepper, Astro, Faust, Bobo, and Zoe. Our puppies went to homes all over New York State, Hartford, Connecticut, and Harrisburg, Pennsylvania. Families even purchased puppies from Toronto, Canada. I guess you could say we were international breeders. God was providing buyers.

LEARNING CURVE

Running a new business always kept us on our toes. We had to learn to be innovative and not stress out about things we didn't anticipate, like how to keep puppies warm. We had to purchase two heat lamps, normally used for chickens, and install each whelping box with a lamp to keep the room at 80 degrees. Newborn puppies can't regulate their body temperatures for the first month, and these heat lamps worked perfectly in our basement nursery during the eight weeks they stayed with us.

I would read about whelping puppies on the internet at night to learn about when their eyes opened, when to start weaning them off milk, and when to start solid food in my blender. I was thankful I could call my mom who had lots of experience whelping puppies.

One day I noticed one of my puppies was throwing up mucus that looked like white cottage cheese. Gross! I was nervous something was wrong with the puppy. I was about to call the vet for advice and knew they would want an emergency vet visit to see the puppy. I didn't want to spend the money on an emergency visit. So I called my mom, and she said puppies sometimes overeat and throw up a little. Boy, I had a lot to learn about puppies! God's strategy for our provision was unusual. My background in music wasn't getting me very far. I had no experience in whelping puppies, but instinct does kick in and I went with my gut on a lot of stuff.

Each puppy was individually photographed every week on the weekday they were born. I would text each family their puppy photo so they could enjoy the weekly growth. Families loved getting the photo and seeing how their puppy was changing each week. The first three weeks puppies' eyes are closed, and they don't really look like a puppy. After their eyes open, families really start to see their pup's personality, and they begin to fall in love. When it is puppy photo day, families are chomping at the bit to see their new photo update, and they all blow up my phone with their sentiments. They were so excited and would always tell me their countdown day until they could hold their puppy in their home.

The photo was a nice personal touch to help families stay connected to their puppy while they waited for the eight weeks until their puppy was ready to come home. We occasionally had a family visit their puppy at around three to four weeks of age. When that happened it was always nice to meet them in person.

Cleaning up the stinky puppy pens in the morning was a chore that Todd and I did together. Teamwork made the process go much quicker, and it was a chance for us to connect about the business and get to know each puppy. They all had names given to them by their families that we were learning to call them by as we got to know their little personalities.

We laid four-by-eight sheets of Styrofoam board down on the cement floor for two reasons: to keep the puppies off the cold floor and to have something soft to staple newspaper to. If we didn't staple the newspaper down, as the puppies wrestled and romped the paper went all over the place. It was usually a mess when we arrived in the morning, but they were happy to greet us. It took two people to clean out the pens and feed them breakfast. We stayed as positive as possible and controlled the grumbling, not wanting to be an Israelite and seem ungrateful for the way God was providing for us. We were committed to get out of the desert and live in the promised land God had for us as quickly as possible.

Our puppies saw our veterinarian, Dr. Hanno, for their six-week vaccinations. I love my vet. We have a great working relationship, and I trust her completely with my puppies. Each puppy had a health check and received the DHPP vaccine and a preventative dewormer. It was a challenge to bring thirteen puppies to the vet in my car, but I used two large Tupperware totes to split the litters up by weight. The totes worked great for transporting puppies in the car.

Dr. Hanno was always so excited to see me and my puppies. She was used to working with sick animals all day long, and my puppies brought happiness to her day. There were many times she would enter my vet room sad and discouraged because she had just lost an animal. It was very hard for her to tell the family that their beloved pet was gone, but when she saw twelve crazy puppies running around the room, it was her chance to love on healthy animals. Puppy therapy we called it. Who doesn't need a little puppy therapy? I think my puppies reminded her of her love for animals and why she became a vet in the first place because there are certainly hard days in the vet world. I believe God can use a puppy to bring happiness and unconditional love to anybody who needs a little lov'in, even to my vet.

Near the end of the eight weeks, I told the kids we were not going to cry when the puppies went to their new homes. We were preparing to let them go emotionally. We loved having the puppies in our home. They were so lovable and friendly, but when it was time to say goodbye to them, we were mentally prepared. The puppies were ready for a larger space to run and play, and we knew each puppy would be loved and cared for. Our puppies go to fantastic homes.

OUR FIRST PAYDAY

When it was time for our puppies to be delivered to their families at eight weeks of age, we offered to deliver them to two large cities near us: Syracuse and Albany, New York. We live two and a half hours from our state capital (Albany) and four hours from New York City. Most of our customers were located in Albany or New York City. The drive to our house to pick up a puppy was a long drive for a family with kids, so we offered to meet halfway at two mall locations, a gesture which people really appreciated.

The morning of delivery we fed our puppies breakfast and loaded them in our car crate to transport them. While we were driving to Syracuse, all the puppies puked everywhere in the crate. I had brought nothing to clean up the mess.

Do not be weary in well doing.

We had no choice but to hand each family their wet, stinky puppy. We felt awful, but our families were so excited to finally be getting their puppy. Our ride home was less than ideal with the stench, but it was our first payday and it was all worth it. Harvest time!

Our first two litters of puppies brought in $15,000 total. We were amazed at God's provision! We tithed $1500. I have to admit writing a tithe check out for $1,500 was a little challenging for us. That was a large amount. However, I knew God was testing our hearts to see if we knew where our provision came from, and we knew we couldn't make puppies. This was a God business. We wanted to honor him with our harvest.

We were so grateful for our unique niche in the marketplace. We passed the money test. We saved twenty-five percent for our quarterly income taxes that Dave Ramsey recommends for home-based businesses and were able to completely fund "baby step three" (three-to-six months of expenses) and start college 529 plans for our kids (baby step four). We were so excited to have our needs met, cash on hand for unexpected expenses, and extra money to throw at the future. Hallelujah! Our foolish days were behind us, and wise days were ahead.

In the house of the wise are stores of choice food and oil, but a foolish man devours all he has.
Proverbs 21:20

CHAPTER SIX

Double Portion

Instead of their shame my people my people will receive a double portion, and instead of disgrace they will rejoice in their inheritance; and so they will inherit a double portion in their land. Isaiah 61:7

While we were whelping our first two litters of goldendoodle pups, my parents called and wanted to talk to us. At that time, we had thirteen puppies in the house and two mamas which seemed like a lot of doodles. We were used to living with only two dogs in the house.

My parents came over and told us they wanted to semi-retire from woodworking and travel with their fifth-wheel camper during the winter months. This lifestyle change for them would not allow for their two goldendoodles to travel with them, so they offered to give them to us free. Our first reaction was shock and we declined the offer. We did not want to live with FOUR dogs. However, both of their doodles, Lucy and Chloe, were still young enough to have puppies.

I remembered the word "start" that God had said when He first told me what the plan would be two years prior. "Start" was a key word we needed to remember in order to know which way to go with our home-based business. "Start" meant there were more dogs to come. The opportunity to have two more goldendoodles was God's plan. However crazy this sounded to us, sometimes God has a plan well beyond anything we can imagine or even understand. Chloe and Lucy were "jars" for us to pour into as well.

It was appealing to have more doodles to breed. BUT...did we want to live with four dogs? Not really. That was A LOT of dogs. We prayed together over a few days, and both of us felt peace from God that this was an open door of opportunity. It actually excited us to think about having more "jars," and we were both in agreement. We adopted Lucy and Chloe. God was providing us with a double portion. We were learning that God always operates in the double portion of more than enough. We were willing to "just say yes!" God's plan was much bigger than we had initially thought.

The widow in 2 Kings 4 went around and got all the jars. The more jars she collected, the quicker she could pay off her debt. I asked Todd the question, "If you had a large hole to fill, would you want two dump trucks or four dump trucks to help fill in the hole?"

He answered, "Four," and we knew what our answer was.

We wanted four dump trucks. So in January 2015, Chloe and Lucy moved in. We were living with thirteen puppies and four mama doodles. It was interesting to say the least. We had the biggest "doghouse" in town.

Do not be weary in well doing.

Our family and friends thought we were nuts. Our educational backgrounds did not line up with this crazy idea. They couldn't understand why we would possibly want to live with four dogs when two were already enough. Four doodles would tie us down to the house even more. We wouldn't be able to travel. We heard it all. But we were tenacious, resilient, and determined. We were leading our family to prosperity no matter what people said. We knew there was a price to pay to win.

We were thinking like entrepreneurs now. God had presented an opportunity to the business for increase, and we were not about to ignore it. It was a business decision. We needed more boats! We needed more jars! We needed more doodle mamas! College tuition was looking enormous. Future expenses like a Ford F150 pickup truck was expensive. And God had provided the double portion to us for free.

We bred Chloe a few weeks after she arrived and Lucy a month later. My days were filled with taking care of thirteen puppies and breeding for our spring litters. I bred four days in a row with our proven stud, Prince. It is hard to know exactly which day will be the correct day of ovulation so I put the dogs together as much as I could around days ten to fourteen of the heat cycle. Talk about being tenacious. I would always breed early in the morning and if they weren't interested, I would try again in the evening. Once they were bred, I did my part and the rest was up to God.

Sow your seed in the morning, and at evening let not your hands be idle, for you do not know which will succeed, whether this or that, or whether both will do equally well.
Ecclesiastes 11:6

SOWING

It wasn't fun breeding in the wintertime. It was cold and sometimes even dark outside. I would sit outside in the freezing snow, with my flashlight, and patiently wait for a "tie" with the dogs. A "tie" is when the stud and mama doodle have "locked up" and insemination has taken place. A "tie" can last up to twenty minutes before they are able to separate. Waiting twenty minutes in the freezing cold was annoying as I huddled to keep warm with my travel coffee mug.

Do not be weary in well doing.

We understood that our prosperity started when we sowed our fields, not the day we harvested. I would pray during breeding and thank God in advance for all the healthy puppies He was making.

"Therefore I tell you, whatever you ask for in prayer, believe that you have received it, and it will be yours." Mark 11:24

We had sixty-three days gestation for Chloe and Lucy's pups. Our first thirteen puppies went to their new homes before our next two litters arrived, which was a nice reprieve for our family. We welcomed the downtime as we had some preparations to do for our next litters. During those two months of waiting, we cleaned out the whelping pens with Clorox, went to the local dump with bags of newspaper trash, and restocked fresh newspaper in anticipation for our spring harvest. The secretary at the newspaper company knew me by name and was always willing to donate their extra papers. It was free paper for me which I loved. The only thing I had to do was sort through and remove all the slippery advertisements. There was always preparation for our next litters.

HARVEST TIME AGAIN

In March Chloe was looking very pregnant. Two days before her delivery due date I went to bed like normal, but around midnight I woke up to a puppy crying. I jumped out of bed and ran to the living room. Chloe had delivered a puppy on my living room carpet! That'll get your adrenaline going.

Do not be weary in well doing.

I yelled to Todd to wake up, start a pot of coffee, and shampoo the rug. I was going to put in a long night helping Chloe deliver her pups. It was inconvenient, but it was harvest time. I refused to complain.

I was able to get Chloe to the basement nursery

to finish whelping her very large litter of eleven puppies. One of the puppies, sometimes called the runt, came out very tiny. With a large litter it is not uncommon to have a much smaller puppy than the rest.

The runt came out of his sac with green meconium all over him. Meconium is the first stool of a puppy. A green puppy is not normal. Once he was removed from his birthing sac, I frantically dried him off, cleared his airway of mucus, and noticed he was still looking green and not breathing on his own. I started rapidly rubbing his chest to get him to start breathing. I began thinking about the money if we were to lose him. $1200 was a lot of money.

I spoke life over him and frantically administered CPR. Gross. I knew I needed to speak out loud and use my authority in the kingdom of God. I was fighting a spiritual battle, and I demanded this puppy to live. I was learning that words hold power to either curse or bless.

The tongue has the power of life and death, and those who love it will eat its fruit.
Proverbs 18:21

I spoke out loud, "This puppy is healthy! Everything I lay my hands to prospers!" After a few puffs from me, he started to breathe on his own. He was alive! I was so relieved. His green coloring lasted a few weeks and finally faded away to show his beautiful crème fur. His family named him Jack and the following year Jack came to stay with us for a few days while the family was on vacation.

I enjoyed seeing him again. He was a healthy, full-grown standard goldendoodle, full of life and love. A month later, Lucy delivered nine doodle puppies. We had a total of twenty puppies. Praise God! During Lucy's whelping, I noticed none of the puppies would nurse on one particular nipple. They were all avoiding it and the nipple was becoming engorged. Once a nipple gets too large, a puppy can't latch on and extract the milk. Avoiding a nipple produces extra milk and pressure builds up. If you are not paying attention to your mama and making sure the puppies are drinking all the milk, a condition called mastitis can develop. Mastitis is an infected mammary gland and requires an emergency trip to the veterinarian clinic to receive antibiotics. I didn't want an emergency vet bill, so I massaged her with a warm washcloth to try and release some milk that was building up pressure.

Do not be weary in well doing.

At first when I touched her, she yelped in pain. She was really sore from the pressure, but slowly the warm washcloth massage released enough milk. Over the next hour of me patiently massaging her, it decreased in size to where I could get a puppy to latch on and start to naturally nurse. I was relieved and thankful to avoid mastitis and antibiotics. God gave me wisdom to solve this unexpected problem at home and avoid the vet. Anytime you can avoid the vet clinic you are saving money. There was never a dull moment with a live animal business.

We were now living with twenty puppies and four mama doodles. I was thankful we had our whelping pens in the basement nursery and not in our personal living space. For the first time, our large dream house seemed the perfect size to be a home-based breeder. We had plenty of extra room to house twenty puppies and not have to whelp them under my dining room table. God's plan was perfect for us. We had plenty of space in our Goliath.

TRUE ASSIGNMENT

I enjoyed the flexibility Willowgreen provided so that I could remain a stay-at-home mom. Mia and I spent a lot of hours in the ballet carpool commute, bonding over movies and music. I loved our time together and with the other ballerinas in the car. The ballerinas were my "car" ministry for years. Carter also enjoyed our unwavering soccer attendance. It was rare if I had to miss a game. I was his biggest cheerleader. I also enjoyed watching our 529 college funds rise.

Crème carpets were now unrealistic living with four doodles. I just couldn't keep them clean with spring and fall mud seasons. Hardwood floors were a must. We were able to replace our crème carpets in the house and upgrade to hardwood flooring.

We also enjoyed the freedom to buy small "wants" and not "needs." Purchasing a pair of shoes or an upgraded iPhone without checking the budget seemed nice. I noticed I didn't check the price of gasoline when I filled up anymore; I just drove to the nearest gas station and pumped my gas. I didn't need to know how much a gallon was. Freedom.

"But seek first his kingdom and his righteousness, and all these things will be given to you as well." Matthew 6:33

ANOTHER PROMOTION

In March we found out there was an opening for school district superintendent at our alma mater, Beaver River, where Todd had been previously employed as the high school principal. It was a promotion, but we didn't want to step out and apply if it wasn't what God wanted for Todd's career. We prayed and asked God for direction. Should Todd apply for the job? The salary increase would be nice, but we were finally at a good place financially and didn't need the money for our monthly budget to run smoothly. That in itself seemed nice to not apply for a job just for the money. The superintendent job came with a lot more responsibility and pressure, so we wanted to be sure it was Todd's purpose.

We were reminded of a conversation Todd had with God a year and a half earlier. At the time Todd was just ending a holiday vacation and was struggling to return to work. Normally it is not a problem for him to return, but this time he was feeling unsettled and unsure why. During worship he asked God, "Why am I unsettled?" and immediately Todd heard a nearly audible voice that said, "You need to lead." Not knowing what was going on, he then asked, "Where?" The response was, "Beaver River," the school where Todd had been a principal two years earlier. At that point the conversation ended, and Todd was in awe of what just happened. Never before had he heard such a clear voice and direction.

God answered us again with His steps for us. We felt peace. Todd applied for the job and while we were on a family walk into town, the phone call came from the board of education. They wanted to offer him the job. He accepted and assumed the role as the new school superintendent. It was a promotion and a blessing to us.

Promotion equals more influence. I believe God was testing our character and integrity earlier in the year with our first puppy profits. Would we be faithful to continue to bring the whole tithe? Could we be trusted with more money? We all have to pass the money test. You will be tested with no money, and you will be tested with money. God rewards those who pass the test. We passed.

> *"No one can serve two masters. Either he will hate the one and love the other, or he will be devoted to the one and despise the other. You cannot serve both God and Money."*
> Matthew 6:2

CHAPTER SEVEN

Goliath Must Fall

"Write down the revelation and make it plain on tablets so that a herald may run with it. For the revelation awaits an appointed time; it speaks of the end and will not prove false. Though it linger, wait for it; it will certainly come and will not delay." Habakkuk 2:2-3

At the end of our first year of breeding we had delivered sixty-three healthy puppies between our four mamas. Our phone was ringing off the hook with buyers wanting a puppy, so I started a call list for families who wanted to be notified when our next litters were coming. We now had a wait list. When I had forty-five people waiting for a goldendoodle, and I knew I wouldn't have forty-five puppies in one litter to meet the demand, we realized we were not at the correct price point. I was amazed that God was bringing so many buyers. The demand for a goldendoodle puppy was greater than my supply. This was a great problem to have as a business owner.

We raised the price of a puppy from $1200 to $1800 in our second year of business. I have to admit I thought $1800 was a lot for a puppy. I wouldn't pay that price for a goldendoodle. I was fearful raising the price would turn buyers away, but God said to me, "I didn't ask you to pay that. I'm asking you to sell at that price; don't limit your prosperity with your poverty thinking. No fear! Sell!"

I began to speak out loud in faith, "Send the buyers, thank You God for all the buyers!"

God knew we could be trusted with more income. We had shown ourselves faithful with a certain amount, and He was ready to take us to the next level. I didn't want to limit what God was trying to get to us (more income) and further His kingdom through our giving. We could give more. God corrected my poverty mindset. We raised the price and began to trust that God was running this successful business, and we were just stewards.

Trust in the Lord with all your heart and lean not on your own understanding; in all your ways acknowledge him and he will make your paths straight. Proverbs 3:5-6

SPIRITUAL WARFARE

Todd and I were also learning through this puppy journey about spiritual warfare. We have an enemy in this life. We can't see him, but he is real. He would love nothing more than to kill, steal, and destroy everything and anything in our life. He hated that we were prospering and starting to affect the kingdom of darkness with our prosperity. When Jesus hung on the cross and the crown of thorns was placed on His head, He was declaring himself King over the system of lack and poverty. We were now walking with one of our weapons, prosperity.

Our enemy, Satan, doesn't care if you have debt. He would love nothing more than for you to stay broke. If you have no money, you have no way to influence the world. It is hard to be a broke giver. How is the body of Christ to feed orphans, build wells for fresh water, or fight sex trafficking with no givers? Everything costs money. Money is an influence and a tool to fight darkness. We were learning that money was a huge part of faith.

The enemy loves to destroy marriages. The number one reason for divorce is money fights and money problems. Todd and I were learning how to fight spiritual battles together as we began to prosper. We knew if the enemy could get us divided and outside our love walk with each other, then the whole thing shuts down. Our prosperity started and finished with a great marriage. We stayed out of strife with each other and with our kids. When we were stressed, tired or "hangry" (hungry with little patience) and said something snippy to another person, we were quick to apologize. Peace and prosperity in our house trumped arguing and pride. We would rather prosper as a family than live with strife. Strife was a dream killer. We worked as a team, all four of us, on the same page day in and day out. We also noticed when our finances were working correctly everybody in the family was happier.

NEW WORTH

By the time our kids were in middle school we had delivered multiple litters, and they were seeing the financial change. They began to talk differently about money. Our kids were correlating the price of a puppy for monetary value instead of the dollar. I would hear them say, "This only cost four puppies," or "That only costs half a puppy." It was definitely an unusual way to think about how much something cost. We wanted to teach our kids that THIS WAS NOT NORMAL. This was a supernatural business. We would laugh at their rationale on purchases, and many times we were astonished by what God was able to make happen for us through the blessing of puppies.

By our second year, we were in a daily routine when we had a litter of puppies at our house. Both of our kids, ages eleven and thirteen, had a lot of responsibility with the business. I would leave the puppies in the middle of the afternoon to pick up ballet carpool, and Carter would check on them when he got off the school bus an hour later. Carter would then be in charge of checking on them (keeping the pen clean) until Todd got home from work. The guys fed dinner to the puppies while we were at ballet, and then in the late evening when I returned home, I would check on them before bed. It was a team effort to run Willowgreen. All hands on deck!

Mia was thriving spiritually and physically with her Christian ballet training, and we knew as parents this was part of our calling to help train Mia for her ministry. So, I made a decision to enjoy the long car rides instead of dreading them. Through the many years of driving ballet carpool, to pass the long, three-hour drive, I would listen to The Dave Ramsey podcast. I loved to listen when families shared their debt-free screams on-air, especially when they were completely debt free including their mortgage. It was so inspiring. I would get a little teary eyed hearing the freedom they expressed in their voices, and I was so happy for them. Their words would speak to my spirit and I would think, "Wow! I want to be completely debt free and scream someday to encourage others." It seemed like a long way off to us. We still had another twelve years on our mortgage. Twelve years. That seemed like forever.

GOLIATH MUST FALL

Our biggest revelation from God came over Christmas break 2015. Lucy went into labor with her second litter while we were hosting our family Christmas dinner! I was downstairs in the puppy nursery helping her deliver, Todd was upstairs cooking a ham, and other family members were busy prepping the food they brought for the meal. It was a full house. It was crazy busy, and I couldn't really be a host. I would come up from the basement and eat a bite of ham dinner and then run back down to the nursery to deliver another puppy. Then my mom would let me eat a few bites of food, and she would go down and check on Lucy. It was comical to see us both up and down from the dinner table.

Do not be weary in well doing.

God's timing for puppies didn't always come at the most convenient times. I was certainly not in control and refused to complain. Just bring in the harvest!

God spoke to me clearly during whelping Lucy's litter. I heard in my spirit, "It is time to take Goliath out, the opportunity is now and will not pass this way again."

I knew exactly what God was saying.

PAY OFF THE MORTGAGE.

WHAT?!

Who pays off their mortgage early?

It was a crazy idea. A GOD idea.

The revelation made sense. I knew Lucy was getting older and heading toward retirement age. She didn't have much time left to have puppies. God was revealing to us *more* of HIS plan, and it was time sensitive. The opportunity would only pass our way *once*.

It never dawned on us to pay off the mortgage early. We never even thought it was feasible. After our first few litters we thought the plan for puppies was to fund college, retirement, and giving. We were content with our financial progress. What was wrong with making a house payment? We realized God was asking us to end the bondage. NO MORE DEBT, which included the house.

God always has bigger plans than we do for ourselves. He wanted us to no longer be slaves and to stretch for the impossible. Wow! It looked like an enormous amount of money to pay off, but He was going to fight this battle for us. We knew this was not our fight.

"With man this is impossible, but with God all things are possible." Matthew 19:26

Our faith began to rise up. Todd and I agreed with what God had told us. We started to speak the Word over our situation. We came into agreement with the kingdom of heaven (there is no debt in heaven). We began to speak out loud thoughts derived from the Scripture:

"We are completely debt free; we are the head and not the tail" (from Deuteronomy 28:13).

"Everything I lay my hand to prospers" (from Deuteronomy 28:8).

"We own the whole estate" (from Galatians 4:4).

We knew that it was finished even before we started paying on the mortgage. We were in agreement for God to move this mountain for us.

"Have faith in God," Jesus answered. "I tell you the truth, if anyone says to this mountain, 'Go throw yourself into the sea,' and does not doubt in his heart but believes that what he says will happen, it will be done for him." Mark 11:22-23

This would be one of Lucy's last litters with us. She was turning seven years of age which was a good time to retire a mama from having puppies. God wanted us to take advantage of having Lucy with us and to start my next assignment. God wanted to take out our Goliath, our $164,000 mortgage.

PREPARING FOR BATTLE

I began studying the word "mortgage." According to Wikipedia, the definition of mortgage is derived from a French law term used in Britain in the Middle Ages meaning "death pledge." It refers to the pledge ending (dying) when either the obligation is fulfilled, or the property is taken through foreclosure.

The root word "mort" means "death." This is where we get the words mortuary, mortal, mortician, mortified, and amortization. We knew God was speaking clearly. Debt was death. Ouch. He no longer wanted us to live with this death pledge. He wanted us financially free and living in the promised land. It was time to let God fight our battle. He was going to fight Goliath using a small and unusual strategy just like David did:

> *David left his things with the keeper of supplies,*
> *ran to the battle lines and greeted his brothers.*
> *As he was talking with them, Goliath, the*
> *ⁱtine champion from Gath, stepped out*
> *ʰis lines and shouted his usual defiance,*
> *ʷid heard it. When the Israelites saw the*
> *ʲey all ran from him in great fear.*

Now the Israelites had been saying, "Do you see how this man keeps coming out? He comes out to defy Israel. The king will give great wealth to the man who kills him. He will also give him his daughter in marriage and will exempt his father's family from taxes in Israel..." Then he [David] took his staff in his hand, chose five smooth stones from the stream, put them in the pouch of his shepherd's bag, with his sling in his hand, approached the Philistine ...

David said to the Philistine, "You come against me with sword and spear and javelin, but I come against you in the name of the Lord Almighty, the God of the armies of Israel, whom you have defied. This day the Lord will hand you over to me, and I'll strike you down and cut off your head ... As the Philistine moved closer to attack him, David ran quickly toward the battle line to meet him. Reaching into his bag and taking out a stone, he slung it and struck the Philistine on the forehead. The stone sank into his forehead, and he fell facedown on the ground. So David triumphed over the Philistine with a sling and a stone; without a sword in his hand he struck down the Philistine and killed him.

I Samuel 17:22-25, 40, 45-46, 48-50

It was time to take out our Goliath with our small stones. Small puppies. Big reward. I had a new assignment with our Willowgreen business. God was ready to do the impossible!

SETTING THE VISION

Hanging in our laundry room were three sheets of paper taped together with a large-shaped thermometer penciled on it. It became our new vision. Along the edge of the thermometer I marked off increments of $2,000 up to $164,000: our goal. As we paid off extra on the mortgage, we would color in more of the thermometer using a green highlighter. The visual helped keep a tally of the amounts we were paying and how much we had to go. It was so encouraging to color in our first lump sum of $3,000 in March when Lucy's puppies left. It was a small step, but we were moving in the right direction. We set the vision in front of us, our thermometer, so a herald could run with it (Habakkuk 2:2). Everybody in our family knew the plan. Eyes on the prize.

As our list of prospective buyers grew, we still had a long list of families waiting for a puppy. Given this, we raised the price again to $2,000 at the beginning of our third year.

Our website and social media were our main sources of reaching the marketplace. Once one puppy was in a community, we had new owners spreading the word for us. They would send in their photos of their new puppy, and I would post them on our Willowgreen Facebook page. Social media was a wonderful way for people to "follow" us and for our business to get free exposure. I enjoyed social networking and running the "people side" of the business. I realized God had given me communication skills to run the business with success. Families who were interested in purchasing a puppy wanted texts and phone calls returned in a timely manner. They wanted their questions answered honestly and quickly. They wanted communication and a relationship. I was really in the people business by selling puppies.

I was always motivated by the thought: "If I were in the market for a goldendoodle puppy, would I like a breeder to do this for me?" If the answer was "yes" then I would do it. For example, I loved dressing up my puppies with bows and bowties for their weekly family photo. My families loved to see their puppy in a bow. Somehow the bows made a puppy even more adorable. People who followed my Facebook page also loved my bows. It was a small gesture of love and care shown to my puppies but paid big dividends. Marketing. Marketing. Marketing!

STEADY EDDIE WINS THE RACE

We were now living WAY below our monthly budget. Todd had resolved to continue to drive his old truck until the house was paid off. If something needed to be fixed, he watched a video online and fixed it himself. Our vision was much bigger than a truck. People continued to pick on him, but we did not care what people thought anymore. We were on a mission.

By April 2016, we had twenty-three puppies at our house at once. It was all hands on deck! We had puppies leaving and puppies coming. In order to hold three litters of puppies at the same time Todd made a third whelping area in our basement. We needed to administrate how to capture the bigger harvest because doodles that live together, heat together. It was a crazy time having three litters here.

Our kids would have friends over, and they would all love to snuggle with the puppies downstairs in the nursery. With that many little dogs, the aroma is not the most pleasant from overnight. One time I heard a kid say, "It smells in here," and I said, "Smells like money to me!" From that day forward our kids would give that reply when anybody said anything about the puppy nursery scent. Once our kids shared with their friends how much each puppy was selling for, they also thought it smelled like money.

DOOR OF OPPORTUNITY

That spring we had the opportunity for our family to travel to Honduras on a mission trip. We were so grateful we had the resources to travel now as a family and give back.

The trip was planned during public school spring break, and we had twenty-three puppies at our house. We had always wanted to take our children on a mission trip while they were in middle school to learn to serve others in a developing country, but I wasn't sure I could leave that many puppies with a doodle house sitter. Who could I trust to come and take care of twenty-three puppies?

I asked two of my teenage relatives if they would be interested in helping me with the business while we were away, and they accepted the challenge. They both had previous experience with raising puppies and I was so thankful God provided us with doodle sitters so we could travel as a family. God was faithful to take care of the details. It was a wonderful trip, sharing the love of Jesus through our vacation Bible school program with orphans in their country. We were learning to trust God with our business while we cared for His business. God is all about the people business, and we were His hands and feet to love and care for them.

After we returned from Honduras, more puppies left our house and we colored in another $17,000 off our mortgage thermometer. Yahoo! Little by little we were seeing progress.

"Little by little I will drive them out before you, until you have increased enough to take possession of the land." Exodus 23:30

God continued to provide buyers for our puppies. We always had a wait list for families who wanted to adopt a puppy from us. I felt the need to ask around for more "jars" like the widow in 2 Kings 4. We needed to pour more jars, but we didn't necessarily want to live with more doodles. We needed to just borrow doodles.

So, I asked my brother Dale and his family if

they would be interested in partnering with me. They also had a standard goldendoodle named Stella who had whelped a few litters in their home. However, Dale's family didn't enjoy the marketing side of puppies or raising them in their home for eight weeks. I had buyers and needed puppies. In order to keep up with the demand for the supply, we needed another mama goldendoodle.

> So they signaled their partners in the other boat to come and help them, and they came and filled both boats so full that they began to sink. When Simon Peter saw this, he fell at Jesus' knees and said, "Go away from me, Lord; I am a sinful man!" For he and all his companions were astonished at the catch of fish they had taken. Luke 5:7-9

Stella lived with my brother, but when it was time to breed and whelp puppies, she came to live with us. I did all the "puppy work," which was birthing and raising the puppies for eight weeks, while Dale kept Stella at his house on the "off" season. It was a win-win for both of us. They received a percentage of the sales for loaning Stella to the business and I received a percentage for raising the puppies. So there were a few months when we were living with five mama doodles. Yes, five.

DIVINE CONNECTION

We ran into an old friend from high school who told us he was getting ready to move to Israel for a three-year placement with the United States

Embassy in Tel Aviv. Since the fourth grade I have had a love for Israel and once picked that country to study and present as a class project. I even decorated a cake like the Israeli flag. We were shocked when he invited us over to visit Israel and to stay with him.

It was a generous invitation. We never thought we would ever be able to afford a trip to the Holy Land. Ever. It was just a dream to travel to Israel. God certainly had a surprise for us! We started to plan our trip for the following spring. We could finally buy airline tickets for our whole family to travel.

Delight yourself in the Lord and he will give you the desires of your heart. Psalm 37:4

KEEP POURING

Our doodles were coming into heat every six to eight months. So when one litter was leaving, we were breeding or expecting puppies from another mama. We kept filling our jars up with oil. There were always puppies here at our house.

At Thanksgiving time Chloe was scheduled to have puppies right around the date we were to have our family dinner. She was still pregnant on the morning of Thanksgiving. I didn't want to leave her home by herself, but I wanted to attend Thanksgiving with my family. I was torn. Sometimes it is hard to know what to do. It would have been easier to stay home where we have all our whelping pens set up, but I really didn't want to waste a family day alone. That wouldn't have been fun. We decided to bring Chloe with us to the dinner and make a whelping area in my mother-in-law's garage.

Once again during a family holiday dinner I was taking a bite of food and running to check on Chloe. No labor. I would run back to the table, eat a few more bites of food, and check on Chloe. No labor. I was working during Thanksgiving dinner. I was trying not to complain about getting disrupted every fifteen minutes from the Thanksgiving table to check on her. I was just thankful we had a harvest coming. Chloe ended up delivering puppies when we got home during the night. It was another all-nighter I pulled to bring in the harvest.

NEW LEVEL

By the end of 2016, our second year of running our home-based business, we had whelped a total of fifty-six puppies. We had colored in another $15,000 in the fall on our mortgage thermometer and bought an SUV with cash. It was wonderful to walk into a car dealership and pay with a cashier's check.

God had paid off $35,000 in one year! He had cut one leg off Goliath. We could see this mountain being *leveled*.

We were enjoying the benefits of walking in faith. Our tithing increased as our income doubled that year. We were passing the new money test. Tithing was a huge part of our success; God was continually testing us to see if money had a foothold in our hearts. We resolved to always tithe. Tithing was an act of worship but also kept us humble and out of pride. We were so grateful for the puppies. It seemed natural to give back to the Creator of all things. We knew we were not making puppies in our own strength. It was a God business. I would tell our kids, "We pay a lot in tithes and taxes," but we wouldn't have it any other way. You can't avoid what I called the two "t's" *and* have God's blessing on your home.

CHAPTER EIGHT

Harvest Time

"For I am going to do something in your days that you would not believe, even if you were told." Habakkuk 1:5

W e continued to have a long waiting list for families who were interested in a puppy, so at the start of 2017 we increased our price again another $500 to $2300. In just two years we were close to doubling the price of a puppy. Another double portion! We continued to tithe on our increase and paid our income taxes. We knew integrity was a huge part of our successful partnership with God.

By the time we landed in Israel in April, we had paid two more large mortgage payments with profits from our four litters born over the winter and spring months. Goliath had lost another leg and an arm; we were enjoying the victories.

If somebody would have told us that we were going to be celebrating our twentieth wedding anniversary in Israel with our children and have half of our mortgage paid off, I would have never believed it. We only had $84,000 to go on our house debt. We could see the light at the end of the tunnel.

ISRAEL

Our public school spring break vacation to Israel happened to be scheduled over Easter. It was a divine moment in time to be able to attend Easter morning services at the tomb in Jerusalem. We worshipped with hundreds of Christians from around the world that day at the tomb. I was completely overwhelmed with God's faithfulness and began to weep. I don't think I sang any words during the worship service. I just wept. Wept with gratitude. Wept with humility. Wept with praise. We were worshipping our Savior together as a family in Jerusalem. I really had no explanation of how we were sitting at the tomb on Easter morning, except for God. He had orchestrated the timing of this whole trip.

Another significant moment happened when our son Carter was able to be baptized for the first time in the Jordan River. He was thrilled and grateful to have this opportunity to share his faith walk and experience his baptism in this special location. Once again, I found myself weeping with gratitude at God's faithfulness as Carter was being baptized in the same spot as Jesus. It was a very special day for our family, and to top it all off, we were able to attend a Hillsong Australia service at the Sea of Galilee in the evening. I was teary eyed again as we sang the song "Oceans" with Hillsong looking over the sea where my Savior walked on water. We serve a BIG GOD! He was blowing us away with divine surprises.

We traveled throughout the country, took our first camel rides in the Negev Desert, floated in the Dead Sea, and visited Ein Gedi, where David hid from King Saul. The Bible was coming alive for us and our children. The biblical locations we read about in our Bible stories were really real locations. We would ask ourselves many times throughout our visit to Israel, "How in the world did we get here?" We were so humbled and grateful for God's puppy provision to allow this amazing trip to even happen. The trip to Israel laid another layer to our faith walk.

POURING SOME MORE

When we returned from Israel, we were breeding for our summer puppies with three mamas in heat at the same time. Between May and July we delivered another twenty-two puppies. When it rains, it pours! The profit from these litters allowed us to build up our emergency fund and begin to save for Todd's pickup truck that we knew we needed to purchase. We were just waiting for the minute his truck would die, and we needed to be prepared to purchase one at a moment's notice. Ford F-150 pickup trucks are expensive. We were buying with cash, so every month that the truck kept running was a good thing.

Once our twenty-two pups left in the early fall, we had eight months with no puppies. We were only able to make our monthly mortgage payment, but we were encouraged and stayed focused. It was hard to be patient during those months. We were used to coloring in large spaces in our mortgage thermometer, but even when we couldn't we kept the vision in front of us. Every month a little bit more was coming off the principal amount left on the mortgage and we would still color in the smaller amounts to keep the dream alive.

Our daily routine still consisted of living day in and day out with four doodles. It was inconvenient to get up in the middle of the night to let the dogs outside. Inconvenient to shampoo rugs when a dog ate grass and puked it up on my living room carpet. And inconvenient to look for our doodles when they ran away chasing a woodchuck, but we knew they were our provision, and we had divine grace to live that way.

HANDWRITING ON THE WALL

During the summer I was starting to feel frustrated with Bella, Gracie, and Chloe when they would run away from our yard through the in-ground fence. The grace was starting to thin as we continued to live with disobedient dogs. They had run multiple times and it was getting old. I was tired of stressing about them when they were gone. This particular escape was the handwriting on the wall we could sense in our spirits.

All three doodles were outside in the yard with me while I raked our grass. I was sure they would stick around if I was outside with them and especially if Bella was nursing nine puppies. However,

I looked up and saw Bella and Chloe running to the back of the property and straight through the inground fence to the neighbor's apple orchard. I called for them to return, but they ignored my screams and ran from me. Ugh!

I was so angry. They would not listen to me at all when they chased wild animals. Anxiety started to build. I had learned through previous escapes that they knew how to return home, but I was nervous something bad would happen to them while they were gone. We had the dangers of hunters and barbwire fencing along our rural area that posed risks for injury. And I certainly didn't want a phone call from the police that they had been hit on the road. Fear was hard for me to fight sometimes.

I assumed Bella would be gone a few hours on her hunt, and I told myself to stay calm. However, when eight hours went by, I knew her nine puppies needed to nurse. The puppies were drinking water so they wouldn't get dehydrated, but they still needed the daily nutrients that nursing provided for their immune systems.

When she didn't return that evening, I needed a plan. How was I going to nurse a litter of puppies? I personally had no milk. I prayed that God would bring Bella home quickly to nurse, but I needed a plan to feed the puppies with supplemental milk in the meantime. I called a breeder friend, Heather, and she told me to purchase puppy formula in a powder form to supplement. I was completely out of my comfort zone. As I was prepping the formula to feed our nine puppies that evening, Bella arrived home. Just in time! I was so thankful to see her return home so she could feed her puppies. God was faithful to return her to us. She was one engorged mama. I'm guessing she was hurting from all that milk and knew she needed to get home and nurse, but Chloe didn't return with Bella. Once again, I felt stressed out and full of anxiety. What had happened to Chloe? Why didn't they return together? Why had they separated? Was she hurt? Was she alive? I was full of questions and no answers. I tried to rest in God that night, but I didn't sleep well. I was praying for Chloe's protection and had decided in the morning to ask the community for help to locate her.

I put a plea out on social media that I was missing a goldendoodle. A local farmer had posted a photo of my two goldendoodles running on the edge of the road near a corn sign by his field. Looking at his photo, I knew it was Bella and Chloe the previous day, so I had a clue where they were running. Maybe Chloe was still near that area. I drove to the exact spot where the photo was taken the previous day and found the corn sign. No Chloe. I started to pray for direction because nothing is hidden from God. He sees everything and knows where everything is. Only God knew where Chloe was. I needed divine help.

I felt the need to continue to drive down the road past a few farms until I thought Chloe couldn't possibly be gone that far from our house. Pulling into the next farm to turn around, I saw a dog sitting on the farmer's front porch. I thought, "Boy that dog looks a lot like Chloe, but it can't be." I looked over a second time and studied the dog because it was so matted and dirty. Sure enough, it was Chloe!

I jumped out of the car and ran up to the porch, "Chloe?!"

The expression on her face was, "What took you so long to come get me? I've been here all night waiting for you!" I could hardly believe I had found her safe and sound. I believe that our tithe was holding her on that porch. The enemy had no right to steal, kill, or destroy her because she was under the promise of the tithe. It was amazing to witness another God moment, promising to protect our business.

I put her in the back of my car and the farmer came out to talk with me. He said he saw two dogs running together across the road in the field all day, and they wouldn't come to him when he called for them. Bella eventually ran home to nurse her puppies, but Chloe was tired from running and decided to sleep on the farmer's porch. I thanked the farmer for allowing her free room and board for the night.

As I was driving home with Chloe, I had so many mixed emotions. I was happy she was found safe, angry that she ran in the first place, and frustrated she didn't stay with Bella to return home. I realized God was preparing us emotionally to re-home them when it was time to stop breeding. We loved our goldendoodles, but they needed a safe and secure yard where they could run freely and safely when they retired. It was better for them to have some place to run with a fenced-in backyard and not an inground fence. They needed safe exercise. We began to pray that God would send us right families when the time was right to rehome them.

RETIREMENT TIME

We were able to rehome Lucy to a wonderful retired couple who was looking for an older goldendoodle to mentor their new puppy. We were also planning to have one more litter of puppies with Chloe. We could feel the grace to live with four dogs was lifting. Our two original goldendoodles, Bella and Gracie, would be turning 6 years old in 2018. All our doodles were nearing retirement age. We had to start thinking about the future of our business. Was God getting done with this business strategy? Did he have something new for us to do? Did we want to raise two more dogs to breed in the future?

After praying about which direction to head, we did not have peace about ending Willowgreen Goldendoodles yet. God once again showed us there is always a double portion in his kingdom.

Instead of their shame my people will receive a double portion, and instead of disgrace they

will rejoice in their inheritance; and so they will inherit a double portion in their land.
Isaiah 61:7

After all, we still had two teenagers in the house, and I was still a stay-at-home mom. We had college tuition in the near future, a ballet internship to pay for, and potential weddings. It still takes a lot of cash to never borrow again. So we purchased two new standard goldendoodle puppies from the same litter in November from a breeder in Pennsylvania. The kids named them Georgia and Ginger. We were living with five doodles now, but we knew it wasn't for long. Bella and Gracie were on their last litters.

CHAPTER NINE

Goliath is Dead

The blessing of the Lord brings wealth, and he adds no trouble to it. Proverbs 10:22

At the beginning of 2018, six puppies were leaving our house, and we welcomed twenty-three from three litters. Our house felt like a revolving door. We were working around the clock, checking on the nursery every hour, making sure puppies were not lost in a corner crying, or a mama hadn't accidentally lain on a puppy, which can be deadly. We were also trying to keep the pens as clean as possible. Over the next eight weeks, we went through a lot of newspaper and washed a lot of whelping blankets. My washing machine could hardly keep up.

Upstairs in our home we were still potty training our new girls, Ginger and Georgia. They were learning what classified as a chew toy and what didn't. We all lost a lot of socks and underwear to chewing. Willowgreen bought plenty of replacement undergarments. I have thrown out rugs, hairbrushes, ballet pointe shoes, and gym shorts from puppy destruction.

Do not be weary in well doing.

We were able to get away and visit Todd's parents over February break in Arizona. Todd's superintendent job, our children's public school breaks, and our business didn't always line up conveniently, but we found a way to work it out and travel as a family. I loved having responsible doodle sitters stay at my house while we were gone. I trusted them completely and was so thankful for good help to administrate our puppy business when we were out of town.

When we returned from Arizona, we delivered our twenty-three puppies to Albany, New York, in March, and with our profit paid another $10,000 off our house. Our thermometer sheet was looking greener and greener. We now had a remaining balance of $58,000. Our mortgage was really going to be paid off!

Our family decided after touring Israel the previous spring that we would like to visit Rome for our next family vacation and continue our Bible tour. Visiting Israel's Old Testament locations had ignited an interest in Rome, Italy, to see parts of where the New Testament was written. It was the perfect continuation. We would be learning and studying about New Testament people and places. There was much to see and do in Rome. It is the location where the Apostles Peter and Paul both ended their ministries and where the early church began. We learned how early Christians were persecuted under the ruling Caesar of the day. We toured the Vatican (where Peter is buried) and visited St. Paul cathedral (where the Apostle Paul is thought to be buried), along with the Coliseum and the Statue of David. It was another dream destination we had always wanted to visit. Once again, we were grateful for the opportunity to travel with our two teenagers and pay cash for it. We were living an astonished life. The good life.

We had purchased tickets for Rome six months before we knew what was going on with our doodle business. We realized that while we were in Italy, Gracie would need to be bred. We didn't want to miss a complete cycle of puppies so I asked my breeder friend, Heather, if she would breed our dogs (she owns the stud). There was a very small window of opportunity to try and breed. We knew we would miss it while we were gone to Italy. It was a blessing to have help running the business while we were overseas.

Be sure you know the condition of your flocks, give attention to your herds. Proverbs 27:23

Stella's and Gracie's spring puppies left when we returned, and we knocked off another $23,000 on our Goliath and tithed on our gross. We were staying faithful to our commitment to continue to honor God. Little by little we were showing ourselves trustworthy.

"Whoever can be trusted with very little can also be trusted with much, and whoever is dishonest with very little will also be dishonest with much. So, if you have not been trustworthy in handling worldly wealth, who will trust you

with true riches? And if you have not been trustworthy with someone else's property, who will give you property of your own?"
Luke 16:10-12

We were down to $35,000 owed on our mortgage by the start of the summer. Goliath had another arm cut off.

TRUSTING THE TIMING

While we were on a camping trip in Ohio for a family reunion, we had planned to extend the trip to visit the Ark Encounter in Kentucky. I knew Bella was due to have puppies the day we were returning from our camping trip. We were cutting it close to be home before labor, but I was hopeful Bella would be a day late for delivery. What was I thinking? I had never missed a labor before, and I didn't think I ever would miss one, but we wanted to attend the family reunion. Poor timing. I was taking a chance that I might not be able to make it back in time.

We were on our last day of camping. My phone rang at 5:00 a.m. I shot out of the camper bed to answer the phone. It was my doodle sitters saying Bella was in labor! There was no way we were packing up a campsite and driving eleven hours home in time for delivery.

It was stressful to not be home at harvest time, but it was out of my control. I had complete trust in my doodle sitters. They had experience delivering puppies and knew what they were doing. The timing of this harvest was a stretch for my faith.

As we were touring the Ark Encounter, my doodle sitter would text with an update as labor was progressing. One, two, three chocolate puppies, four, five, six chocolate puppies, seven, eight... I couldn't believe it was such a large litter because she was getting older. Finally, at the end of the day we had a total of nine healthy chocolate goldendoodles. Bella did a great job all by herself.

My sitters received a bonus pay for going above and beyond the call of puppy sitting. They did a great job through labor and delivery. Once again, the harvest sometimes doesn't come at a convenient time, but we continued to persevere and not complain. God's timing is always perfect, even though it may not always seem that way at the time.

Over that summer, we received a call from a woman who was looking for a retired goldendoodle to adopt. She already had adopted one goldendoodle but was looking for an older companion for her puppy to play with. I told her we would have a retired goldendoodle named Chloe in the fall ready to rehome. She came to visit us and met Chloe to see if she was a good fit with her kids and puppy. It was perfect for her situation. God had provided the wonderful home we had been praying for. He knew every detail in our business, and it was becoming easier to rest in that truth.

GOLIATH IS DEAD

By September 2018 we were steps away from killing Goliath. Our fourteen summer puppies helped us finish paying off the mortgage. What should have taken us twelve years in the natural to pay off, God paid off in seventeen months. Months! AMAZING!

We went to our local bank and asked for a cashier's check of $8,000 to send in our FINAL mortgage payment. As we finished up with the bank teller, she said to us, "Now that you own your house, would you be interested in a lake house?"

"No thank you," we said, "we don't borrow money." We laughed all the way to the car. We were headed to the promised land. FREEDOM. The feeling was nothing like anything we had felt before.

We are more than conquerors through him who loved us. Romans 8:37

Goliath was dead. God had conquered it and cut its head off. He had killed our mortgage with a unique strategy in the marketplace. We were amazed at the faithfulness of God. In less than two years we were COMPLETELY debt free including our house. Hallelujah!

"If you hold to my teaching, you are really my disciples. Then you will know the truth, and the truth will set you free." John 8:31-32

SCREAM IT OUT

We called the The Dave Ramsey Show when we returned from the bank and lined up our debt-free scream for February 2019 on the live talk radio show. We couldn't wait to scream with our kids and meet Dave Ramsey. Our celebration was planned for February 22, 2019, in Nashville, Tennessee, live on air. We were beyond excited. It was certainly a financial milestone to share together because it took all four of us as teammates to run with our vision. We had walked out God's plan for financial peace, and we wanted to encourage others on their debt-free journey. We were called to be salt and light in a dark world. We knew we needed to share our amazing story with Dave Ramsey listeners.

Anyone who receives instruction in the word must share all good things with his instructor.
Galatians 6:6

The year 2018 finished with fifty-nine total pups delivered and a whopping total of 211 puppies since we started Willowgreen Goldendoodles. God's provision was abundant. If you would have told me two years prior that we would have 211 puppies come through my home, I would have never agreed to start the business. That number would have seemed overwhelming to me and a lot of work. I'm thankful God doesn't share all His details with us at the beginning, or we won't probably do a lot of things. His faithfulness, however, superseded our expectations and we had another abundant year.

We now had money in our monthly budget to be generous. Very generous. It was fun to give money when you have some to share. We have several ministries that are near and dear to our hearts. We became monthly partners with an orphan ministry in Honduras and the television ministry, *Fixing the Money Thing,* that had impacted our financial journey. We were able to start leaving extravagant tips with our servers on Christmas Eve, which has become a beloved family tradition. This past year, as we were running to our car to leave the restaurant, our waiter caught us in the parking lot to thank us. His smile was the highlight of our Christmas that year.

"It is more blessed to give than to receive."
Acts 20:35

It felt good to give. It felt freeing to give. Money became a tool for us to be a blessing and share the love of God. Life was not all about us anymore. Life is not all about you. When you are free financially, it is time to listen to God about what He wants you to do with it. Some is for eating and some is for giving. Some is for saving and some for investing. Our whole family, including our kids, have learned the four ways to handle God's money. When you are obedient and follow God's ways of handling money, you will prosper. You will have more than enough to be generous on every occasion.

"Give, and it will be given to you. A good measure, pressed down, shaken together and running over, will be poured into your lap. For

with the measure you use, it will be measured to you." Luke 6:38

Our retirement funds were well on their way, and we were starting to build wealth. You can actually have your money work for you. What a novel idea. The great Albert Einstein once said, "Compound interest is the eighth wonder of the world. He who understands it, earns it ... he who doesn't ... pays it."

Now that the mortgage was done and we were completely debt free, we were full steam ahead for our future goals: college tuition, funding our retirement accounts, and extending our giving to missions abroad. We also wanted to continue traveling with our teenagers while they were still living with us. We planned another trip to the Middle East countries of Egypt, Jordan, and Israel for our family spring break. Our friends in Israel invited us to meet them in Cairo, Egypt, to tour the pyramids and see the land where the Israelites were held in captivity. It was another special trip we believe God was correlating with our debt-free journey. We had come out of Egypt (debt) and were crossing into Canaan (our promised land).

CHAPTER TEN

His New Plan

"Forget the former things; do not dwell on the past. See, I am doing a new thing! Now it springs up; do you not perceive it?"
Isaiah 43:18-19

Our two new doodles, Georgia and Ginger, turned one year old in the fall. We noticed over the summer they were not growing. We were beginning to wonder if Mia's prayers were answered; she wanted them to stay puppy sized. Usually by one year old a puppy is fully grown, weighing between fifty-five to sixty-five pounds, but our little doodles were full grown at twenty-five and thirty-five pounds. They were definitely not standards. What did we buy?

I was very confused, so I called the breeder in Pennsylvania to inquire about our doodles and to ask about the size of the stud he used. He told me I bought mini goldendoodles. Surprise. I had no idea we were buying minis and not standards. We accidently got the wrong size. We had been breeding only standard F1b goldendoodles. There was no way that our mini mamas were going to be bred to a standard poodle in the natural. It wasn't physically possible to even get a "tie" with the height difference, let alone carry a large litter of standard puppies in their wombs. We were in new territory. My plan was to continue to breed standard golden-doodles. God's plan was not. He had changed strategies on us without us even knowing. We were going to be breeding mini goldendoodles now. Our business partner, God, seemed to be throwing us a curve ball.

I was thankful Heather owned a miniature chocolate poodle stud, called Charlie, that we could use for our new mini mamas. Finding a stud is half the battle when you are breeding for puppies. Our "mini" plot twist came with more provision: minis are more expensive than a standard. Market price for a miniature doodle was between $3,300-$3,500 for a puppy. God was moving us into another market niche. He always knows where the money is.

Our new "line" of mini goldendoodles generated a lot of buzz on our social media page. We told our Facebook followers that we would be breeding for mini puppies in 2019. Unbeknownst to us, there was a huge demand for this size goldendoodle. We learned that renters who live in New York City have a forty-pound weight limit on pets in apartment buildings. Minis were a perfect size for city living. Who knew? God did. Also, the smaller weight size was appealing to families with smaller children and elderly couples looking for a smaller pet to take care of. We started our minis at $3300 and raised our standards to $2500 at the new year. God was up to something new.

Our Bella and Gracie were in their last year breeding. We didn't know if we should breed for standard or mini puppies, but the demand for minis was incredible. We had a slight problem, though, as Bella and Gracie were standard size with long legs. Our miniature poodle stud, Charlie, would need a step ladder to get the job done. It was impossible in the natural.

We had a decision to make. Do we continue breeding standard goldendoodles and stay in the familiar, or do we take a risk and start something new? It was easy to get into fear. What if our minis couldn't have puppies? I knew I had a proven stud. We prayed about the direction we should go for the next year, and we both had peace about following God. He was changing up the business strategy to do minis with Ginger and Georgia, so why not try Bella and Gracie as well.

We had a huge call list of families waiting for a mini, so we took the risk and decided to breed Bella with Charlie using artificial insemination (A.I). An A.I. is a medical procedure only our veterinarians could perform. It involves expensive blood tests to know when your mama is ovulating. The veterinarians like to do the procedure at least twice, if not three times, to get the best results. There is a lot more work and timing involved and sometimes an A.I. doesn't work. Humans are not as good at breeding as God is. We took our first step out of the boat and went ahead with the procedure.

Bella's A.I. was a financial risk for us at $400.

We were being stretched. I had new vocabulary words to learn and new veterinarians to meet at our clinic. Not all vets can even perform artificial insemination, so it was a miracle that the correct vet was at the clinic the day we needed the procedure done. We knew God was calling us to do a new thing and He worked out the details.

> *"Enlarge the place of your tent, stretch your tent curtains wide, do not hold back; lengthen your cords, strengthen your stakes. For you will spread out to the right and to the left."*
> Isaiah 54:2-3

The nice thing about A.I. is you know exactly which day to breed. There is no guessing like breeding dogs in the natural. Our vet called with the blood work and told us, "Today is the day; go get Charlie!" I stopped what I was doing, jumped in the car, and drove to get him. While trying to settle the mop of curly brown poodle hair on my lap, I raced back to the vet clinic as fast as I could. The vet proceeded to perform the A.I. The whole process from phone call to the actual procedure took about an hour. When it is "go time" one must "go."

Our first litter of minis was potentially arriving in March. We knew enough now about sowing into the kingdom for items we were believing God to bring into our life. We sowed a seed into a ministry that had good ground and came into agreement for a white Ford F-150 truck from this litter. I had faith for a litter of mini puppies, and Todd was believing for the double portion. It was going to take a large litter to purchase a truck.

"Therefore, I tell you, whatever you ask for in prayer, believe that you have received it, and it will be yours." Mark 11:24

We believed we had a litter of minis coming. We couldn't see puppies in the natural when we sowed and agreed, but we knew we had puppies on the way. Our faith was activated. During Bella's gestation, I would lay my hands on her belly and say, "We have a lot of healthy puppies coming; everything I lay my hands to prospers" (Deut. 28:8).

DEBT-FREE SCREAM

While waiting for our mini litter to arrive, during our winter break from school we flew to Nashville, Tennessee, to share our debt-free scream on The Dave Ramsey Show. We were excited to be making a huge family memory together celebrating paying off our mortgage on national radio. The opportunity to share our story and encourage listeners to persevere in their debt-free journey was priceless. Several years of listening to others call in with their debt-free screams made us hungry to stay committed to our journey, and we wanted to give back.

As iron sharpens iron, so one man sharpens another. Proverbs 27:17

We arrived with our matching black T-shirts I had made on my Cricut machine two weeks prior that said, "Tithe it." We were scheduled to scream during the second hour on the live show and enjoyed the free coffee and cookies while we waited. With anxious, full bellies and coffee in hand, we put headsets on to scream live in front of seven million people.

When it was time to go live on air, the host walked us through what questions Dave would be asking us. It was equal parts humbling and daunting to share our story with the world. I felt vulnerable; up to this point I had not shared our financial journey with even my mom. Once we screamed, during the commercial break Dave came out to greet us in the lobby and we took our photo with him. He was so kind and graciously let me show him my mortgage thermometer that made the journey with us. He autographed, "Dave Ramsey, Romans 12:2, Transformed!"

Our family legacy was forever changed. The abundant life was now our life. It was a new reality for us.

(If you would like to view our live debt-free scream on The Dave Ramsey Show, visit the following link: https://youtu.be/cspsBTBR5Gs. Our interview begins at the 1:29:20 hour marker.)

POURING NEW OIL

When we returned from Nashville, Bella was looking enormous. We knew we would have puppies, but Bella was looking larger than I was expecting. The A.I. procedure proved successful. I was not believing for a large litter because I was told older mamas typically have smaller litters. But nothing in our divine business was typical. God can do the impossible. And He can make as many puppies as He wants to.

We delivered our first litter of mini goldendoodles in March. Bella had labored all through the night and by 6:00 a.m. she had delivered eleven chunky, warm puppies. I was baffled at the harvest. Overtired from sitting beside her through the entire twelve-hour labor, I went to bed. As per usual, Todd got up in the morning to check on Bella. Five minutes later I awoke to him exclaiming, "I just counted twelve puppies. Twelve!"

I shot out of bed, "What?! No way! That's your faith for the double portion; that's your truck!"

Twelve mini puppies at $3300 each was more than enough for Todd's truck. God did the impossible. Bella's last litter was one of her biggest. The harvest was plentiful.

Our mini puppies were born about the same size as a standard puppy, but by five weeks of age they were not nearly the size of a standard puppy. We had all different colors as well: caramel, chocolate, and crèmes. They were absolutely adorable.

DIVINE TRIP

We lined up our doodle sitters again for our spring break trip to Israel, Jordan, and Egypt. Our five-week-old mini puppies would still be home while we were traveling. There is a lot of work during weeks five through eight when puppies are excessively eating, pooping, and playing. Once again, it wasn't the best time to leave a litter of puppies, but the trip's timing couldn't be changed. I was always apprehensive about leaving puppies and could quickly start to fear, especially about leaving my first litter of minis, but I trusted my doodle sitters to take really good care of them.

While waiting in the Cairo, Egypt, airport to board for Amman, Jordan, I received a phone call from home. It was our doodle sitter, frantically talking. We didn't have a good phone connection, but I could make out that something was wrong with our mini pups and a few of them were lethargic. I told her to take them to the veterinarian's office as soon as it opened at 8:00 a.m. We hung up, and our family immediately began to pray in the airport for healthy puppies. I didn't like being that far away from home. It was easy for me to get into fear and anxiety. Prayer was our only weapon. We were praying for healing. I needed to trust God that He had this litter under His care. We thanked Him in advance for all our healthy puppies. Peace washed over us and we boarded our flight for Amman.

As our plane ascended Cairo, Egypt, and flew back into Amman, Jordan, the flight went directly over the Sinai Peninsula. I sat in amazement at what God had done for us through our puppy business. I felt at peace. Looking out my window down at all the desert sand, I could picture the Israelites walking around down there, headed to the Promised Land through Jordan. Just like us, they chose to follow God, left the land of bondage (Egypt), and headed to their inheritance in the Promised land of Israel. We were traveling the same path the Israelites did.

Later that evening my sitter called me in Jordan to let me know the puppies were just dehydrated, and the vet gave the whole litter fluids. It was nothing serious, but if they hadn't received the fluids it could have been life threating. Because Bella was in the process of weaning them, she wasn't lying down anymore for them to drink her milk. The mini puppies were too short to reach for milk and hadn't learned how to drink water on their own. This was a new problem for me as a breeder. I needed wisdom.

For the Lord gives wisdom, and from his mouth come knowledge and understanding. He holds victory in store for the upright, he is a shield to those whose walk is blameless, for he guards the course of the just and protects the way of his faithful ones. Proverbs 2:6-8

I was so relieved to hear it was nothing serious. Thank You, God! We had all these puppies spoken for, and I didn't want to have to call a family with sad news. I never had this issue of dehydration come up with standard puppies. They were tall enough at that age to stand on their hind legs and reach up to drink milk. So over the phone I talked my doodle sitter through our plan to teach the puppies how to drink water and stay hydrated. I told her to place a shallow water bowl on the floor in the center of the whelping pen so all the puppies could see it better. If the bowl was more visible, I was hoping the puppies would be curious and come check out the water. We had more water on the floor from the puppies splashing around in the water bowl, but it was worth the mess to have hydrated pups. There was certainly a learning curve to having mini puppies and a standard mama.

When we entered the security checkpoint from Jordan to Israel and drove back to Tel Aviv, we had time to visit the Valley of Elah, where David killed Goliath. It was a special location we wanted to visit as it symbolized a significant part of our debt-free story. God used this biblical account to teach us how He fights our battles in strange and unique ways.

As we parked alongside the road to the Valley of Elah, I could hardly contain my excitement to be there. I just wanted to get out of the car and start walking the fields of wheat. We found a path down to a small creek bed where David would have picked up his small stones in his sling to throw at Goliath. As I walked along the field and let the wheat flow through my hands, I began to weep. I was so grateful to be there. I was overwhelmed with emotions of gratitude. I couldn't believe God gave us the opportunity to visit Israel again and witness this epic biblical location and see with our own eyes where this battle took place. God was surely walking along with us; the sun was shining, and the gentle breeze was refreshing. I have a piece of wheat from the Valley of Elah in my house, and every time I look at that stalk it brings me back to that special day in the picturesque valley. I'm reminded of God's faithfulness to us. Just like David, we had killed our Goliath with God's help.

We were finally able to purchase a Ford F-150 truck with cash from this litter. Todd had been patiently waiting for the right moment, and our house was paid off. It was time. We went to a local dealership looking for a white truck that we had sowed for. They didn't have one we wanted so we bought a grey Ford F-150 with cash. It wasn't exactly what we were hoping for, but it was still a nice truck. Two months later, while driving to work Todd rear ended a lady and totaled his truck. Thankfully, neither person was injured, but both vehicles were totaled. I asked God, "Why did that happen? Todd waited two years for that truck. We paid cash. We did it Your way."

God said, "You sowed for a white pickup truck. That one was grey. I was under no obligation to protect that truck." Woah. We learned our lesson. Be careful what you sow for. We were specific and we didn't think God was that specific.

Our car insurance gave Todd more than what we had paid for the grey truck. We actually made money on the wreck. I don't recommend that way to make money. He returned to the same dealership with his insurance check and this time bought a white one, the color he really wanted. This one is protected!

Our faith was challenged again. God was showing us we don't have specific things because we don't think to ask.

> *"Which of you fathers, if your son asks for a fish, will give him a snake instead? Or if he asks for an egg, will give him a scorpion?"*
> Luke 11:11

Every once in a while we get an ebony-colored puppy, and for whatever reason our families are not looking for this color. The black puppies are always the last to be adopted, which is confusing because they are adorable. However, I guess if you are looking for a goldendoodle, you want the "golden" color. I asked God about this one day:

"Why do You send us black puppies?"

"Karla, you only ask for healthy puppies. I send you whatever I want to, but I have no obligation to send certain colors."

I was starting to get it. The kingdom of God works the same way as the natural realm. If my daughter asked me for a healthy puppy, I would find a healthy puppy. If she asked me for a caramel puppy, I would get her a caramel puppy, not a crème one, not an ebony one. God is the same way.

We sowed a seed into the kingdom of God and came into agreement for two litters of either caramel or crème mini goldendoodles, with no ebony puppies. I was stretching my faith. We delivered a harvest of eighteen from the first two litters, all either caramel or crème, with no ebony, just like we had asked for. God was faithful.

We enjoyed another full summer with three mini litters here at the same time from my brother's standard goldendoodle, along with Ginger and Georgia. The weaning process from milk to water went much better this time. We stayed hydrated.

When it came time to breed Ginger for her first litter of mini puppies, I went and picked up Charlie for the "job." I was expecting a quick natural tie because they were both the same height. Well, he was too short. All he needed was one extra inch of height to get a tie naturally with Ginger. So, I asked Todd to make me a little platform for him to stand on to get the correct height for him. It was made out of plywood and two-by-four wood. We called it the "love lift." There were certainly some good laughs over making this ramp! It worked like a charm though; Ginger had ten mini goldendoodles naturally with Charlie.

STOP POURING

Our last Gracie litter was also during this summer. I knew she was getting too old to have puppies. She wasn't looking very big either. I never know how many puppies we are going to have.

Her first puppy came out normal, and I could feel at least another puppy. I was expecting an hour to go by for the second puppy, which is normal labor, but after the fourth hour I was getting nervous. She wasn't pushing or in distress. I was confused with her slow labor and trying to remain calm and speak life. By the time eight hours had gone by, I thought we had lost the puppy. That was just too much time inside the womb without delivery.

She seemed tired and not interested in pushing at all. I didn't know if a puppy was stuck, and now time was not on my side. I called the vet and told them Gracie was in active labor; I had delivered one puppy, but I could feel another one. The vets were very concerned and wanted me to come in immediately for an emergency C-section, which is expensive and causes a longer recovery time for a mama. However, I drove to the vet's office with one newborn puppy wrapped in a towel and Gracie in active labor in the backseat of my car.

Do not be weary in well doing.

Once they had me in a room, we did an x-ray, which showed there were two more puppies. They were in perfect location and completely protected in their sacs. I was so thankful. Everything looked normal. Nobody was stuck. I was surprised we had two puppies. I brought blankets for Gracie to lie on the vet floor with her puppy that was already born. One of the vets came in and told me I was scheduled for the operating room as soon as the first surgery was done. He left the room, and while we were waiting for the surgical room to be available, Gracie pushed out a second healthy puppy on the dirty vet office floor!

"Somebody bring me some towels!"

I was so thankful the puppy wasn't stuck, and we cancelled the emergency C-section. I went home with two puppies, Gracie, and no vet bill. An hour later Gracie delivered her third puppy in her whelping pen. Praise God.

Our summer was crazy with a full house of mini puppies. At a grand total of twenty-two, it was a puppy palooza. Our jars were overflowing.

We knew these litters would be the last for Bella and Gracie. They had certainly earned their keep at our house, but we knew God wanted them to be rehomed for safety and health reasons. They needed a fenced-in yard to play safely, not an inground fence. I prayed that God would show us the right families for our girls to be adopted into.

We had two former Willowgreen families inquire about our mini goldendoodles as a second pet for their family, so I knew they were already interested in another doodle. When they decided to not adopt a mini, I thought they might be interested in adopting the parent of their puppy. One family had a Bella puppy named Molly, and the second family had a Gracie puppy named Olivia. I reached out to both families and asked them if they would be interested in adopting the mama of their puppy at no charge. The only requirement we asked was that they have the mamas spayed to ensure a long, healthy life.

I knew it was a bit of a shock to receive a phone call from me and hear the question, "Would you ever be interested in adopting Molly's mama, Bella? We are looking to rehome her with one of her puppies to a wonderful retirement home."

It was a big decision for each family to think over, but they both agreed to take them. They both felt honored that we would even consider calling them. It was my heart's desire for Bella and Gracie to live with former Willowgreen families whom I could trust. God made a way for this all to happen. We love getting photo updates from both families and enjoy hearing how Bella and Gracie are doing. They are loved and spoiled (more so than with me), which warms my mama heart.

OUR ABUNDANT LIFE

As we enter the next year, we are planning for three litters in February-March 2020. Coming off a quiet fall and Christmas season, our home will once again be filled with puppies to love on and bless other families. The harvest will be arriving all at once. We have a lot of work ahead of us, but it is well worth it.

We have come a long way from living paycheck to paycheck. We are living our real Cinderella story now. Our hearts have gone through major surgery while fixing the money thing. Our trust and faith in God have grown immeasurably, and He can trust us with more responsibility. Through our journey to reach a debt-free life, we have learned how the kingdom of God operates. He is fighting our daily battles. We can rest in knowing He won the ultimate battle on the cross. He died for ALL of our debts. He wants the abundant life for you. He died for it.

The world will tell you that you're all on your own, and it's up to you to make it all happen. That's a lie. We understand now that God delights in taking good care of His children. You are invited to His table. The invitation is yours. It's simple; just accept. Surrender. His plans for you are good. He is a good Father; let Him take you on your faith journey. It is well worth it.

Looking ahead, our children will be leaving our home soon and pursuing their own dreams. We ask God about His future purpose and plans for all four of us, and we hear in our spirits,

"How many puppies do you need? I'm unlimited."

Hallelujah! Financial peace and endless provision.

Our future holds great optimism. This new season of living and giving is the abundant life. Mia will be graduating from high school in 2020 and auditioning with Light of the World Ballet, a company to start her ballet ministry. Todd is testing for his personal pilot's license, and Carter has plans to study pre-med in college. For me, my next mission was to write our story, to share my family's testimony of His faithfulness. We are ready when God opens up a new door of opportunity. We are ready to listen for our next plans.

We are ready for DESTINY!

Final Thoughts

You may recall our story began with these opening questions:

Can you have it all?

A thriving marriage.

Children who walk in peace with one another.

Generous finances.

Excellent health.

A dream home.

Can you have an abundance in all these areas?

The simple answer is "Yes." Our journey to financial peace brought abundance to all these other areas as well. As we learned how to listen to God regarding our finances and get on the same page as a couple, we began to communicate better in our marriage. Better communication made for a thriving marriage. We started to dream together about our future. We enjoyed being around each other, and our children enjoyed spending time together as a family. Our children saw us emulate a healthy Christian marriage. Are we perfect? No, but our relationships with each other are stronger and more transparent than they were before we started this faith journey. Our kids share a special connection, and they love to share their lives with each other.

We have allowed God to change our hearts to give more generously within our home, community, nation, and world. As we continue to walk with God, we serve His kingdom. We are able to look outside our own small reality to help others in need.

With all that said, the best part of this whole journey was growing our personal walks with God. My entire family has pressed into ALL that God has for us. Our children are serving God. We all have witnessed a good, good Father in so many areas of our lives. Our spiritual walks have grown immeasurably throughout this process, and we are grateful for the lessons we have learned as disciples of Christ. This is the true abundant life. Our hearts were changed more into the image of Christ, and that is the ultimate destination.

He who pursues righteousness and love finds life, prosperity and honor. Proverbs 21:21

"Fixing The Money Thing" TV Show with Gary Keesee

Sharing Our Story

During Lucy's litter we received a call from Gary Keesee's television producers asking us to share our story on their television show: Fixing the Money Thing. We were humbled and honored to tell others how we overcame. They sent a film producer to our home in January, which worked out perfectly because we had puppies at our house during that time to film. Once our story aired on the television program in the spring, I received several emails from families who were interested in learning about the puppy business. Our story inspired them to pursue their own "oil." I am currently mentoring several ladies around the United States who have started their own puppy businesses at home to achieve financial freedom. This is something I love to do. God certainly had bigger plans for us than I had.

If you would like to watch our televised testimony, go to: www.faithlifechurch.org and look in the message archives for the April 28, 2019 on the "The Difference a Year Can Make" by Pastor Gary Keesee. The video insert on our story begins around the 20:14 minute mark.

Contact Information

You may contact the author, Karla Green,
at the following email address:

tkmgreen@hotmail.com
www.willowgreenministries.com

Individuals and church groups may order books
from Karla Green directly, or from the publisher:

Deeper Revelation Books
P.O. Box 4260
Cleveland, TN 37320 423-478-2843
Website: www.deeperrevelationbooks.org
Email: info@deeperrevelationbooks.org

Photo Gallery

"But those who hope in the Lord will renew their strength. They will soar on wings like eagles; they will run and not grow weary, they will walk and not be faint." Isaiah 40:31

Our wedding December 1997

Our first two goldendoodles, Bella and Gracie, with Carter and Mia

Whelping Bella and Gracie's first two litters in our kitchen

Building our puppy nursey

Newborn goldendoodles, we call a puppy pile

Mama goldendoodles: Chloe, Stella, Bella and Gracie

Mini goldendoodle puppies

Playtime outside

The Garden Tomb, Jerusalem, Israel

Puppy bath time in the kitchen sink

Mini goldendoodles,
Georgia and Ginger

Mini goldendoodle puppies
playing with Carter

Our debt free scream on The Dave Ramsey Show

Valley of Elah, Israel (where David killed Goliath)

Our Goliath (dream home)

Pyramids, Cairo, Egypt

Bella, Gracie, Ginger and Georgia on squirrel patrol

A litter of mini goldendoodles

Puppy snuggles

Enjoying Mother's Day